PREHISTORIC PEOPLES

PREHISTORIC PEOPLES

DISCOVER THE ANCIENT WORLD
OF THE FIRST HUMANS

PHILIP BROOKS

ARMADILLO

This edition is published by Armadillo, an imprint of Anness Publishing Ltd,
108 Great Russell Street, London WC1B 3NA; info@anness.com

www.armadillobooks.co.uk; www.annesspublishing.com; twitter: @Anness_Books

Anness Publishing has a new picture agency outlet for images for publishing,
promotions or advertising. Please visit our website www.practicalpictures.com
for more information.

A CIP catalogue record for this book is available from the British Library

Publisher: Joanna Lorenz
Produced by Miles Kelly Publishing Limited
Project Editor: Raje Airey
Design: Angela Ashton

PICTURE CREDITS
The publishers would like to thank the following
artists who have contributed to this book:
James Field (SGA); Richard Hook (Linden Artists); John James (Temple Rogers);
Stuart Lafford (Linden Artists); Shane Marsh (Linden Artists);
Terry Riley; Martin Sanders; Peter Sarson; Rob Sheffield; Sue Stitt;
Mike White (Temple Rogers); John Woodcock.
All maps are by Steve Sweet (SGA)
The publishers wish to thank the following
for supplying photographs for this book:
Page 8 (B/L) AKG Photo; 9 (B) Erich Lessing/ AKG London; 11 (B) Mary Jelliffe/
Hutchison Library; 16 (B/R) E.T. Archive; 18 (B/R) E.T. Archive; 26 (B/L) The Stock
Market; 28 (B/R) The Stock Market; 35 (B) Mary Jelliffe/ Hutchison Library; 38
(T/R) Erich Lessing/ AKG London; 41 (B) Ancient Art & Architecture Collection; 44
(T/R) English Heritage Photo Library; 52 (M) English Heritage Photo Library; 55
(T) English Heritage Photo Library; 58 (T/R) English Heritage Photo Library;
61 (B/L) Southwell/ Hutchison Library.
All other photographs from Miles Kelly archives.

Manufacturer: Anness Publishing Ltd,
108 Great Russell Street, London WC1B 3NA, England
For Product Tracking go to: www.annesspublishing.com/tracking
Batch: 7469-23565-1127

CONTENTS

Introduction

IN THIS SECTION WE WILL LOOK BACK to the very beginnings of the human story. It starts at a time when people lived in caves and sheltered under cliffs, when the only tools were made of stone, when everyone had to hunt or forage for their own food, when clothes had to be made from animal skins. There were no cities, no large buildings, none of the comforts of modern life, and no one had worked out how to write.

The term "prehistory" means the time before people were able to write their history down. Writing developed at different times in different parts of the world, so the date when the prehistoric period ended varies from one place to another. In Mesopotamia in South-west Asia, for example, writing came around 3000BC. In western Europe by contrast, widespread use of written scripts coincided with the Roman conquerors around 3,000 years later.

Prehistoric life can sound grim. Life was hard, travel must have been difficult, and many people died young without the benefits of effective medicine. Yet the period sees the beginnings of the very things that make humanity what it is today. Technology was simple, but it made possible amazing monuments like Stonehenge. Artists had only basic materials, yet they produced masterpieces on their cave walls. People cared for their

▲ HOMINIDS
The first human-apes appeared about four million years ago in Africa. They came down from the trees where they lived and began to walk on the ground on two legs. Scientists call them australopithecines.

▼ KEY DATES
How humans and human society developed in different parts of the world.

▼ CAVE ART
It seems that humans have always felt the urge for artistic self-expression. During the Ice Age, people lived in caves. Wall paintings from that time show people's skill in making their homes bright and attractive.

	4–1 MILLION YEARS AGO	1MYA–400,000BC	400,000–30,000BC	30,000–12,000BC
AFRICA	Early hominids, the first human-apes, are alive in eastern Africa.	*Homo erectus*, a type of early human, use stone handaxes as a multi-purpose tool.	*Homo sapiens*, humans, appear in various places south of the Sahara.	
MIDDLE EAST & ASIA		*Homo erectus* are established in both Java and China, and have probably mastered the use of fire.	Neanderthals and "modern" humans are living side by side in Mesopotamia.	Rock painting
EUROPE		First known settlement of *Homo erectus* in Europe.	Neanderthals and "modern" humans are present, and may breed, but Neanderthals die out.	Europe freezes in the Ice Age. Artists make great cave paintings in France and Spain.
AMERICAS	*Skull of* Homo habilis	*Sabre-toothed cat*		The first settlement of North America begins as men and women cross the Bering land bridge from Siberia.

MYA = Million years ago

▲ MAMMOTH
SHELTER
*Homes were built from
whatever materials
were available. Remains
of mammoth bones
suggest they were used
to build massive shelters
almost 3m/10ft high.*

▶ FISH CARVING
*After the Ice Age, food
supplies were
much better.
Fish carvings
found in
Europe
suggest that
fish had
become part of
the staple diet.*

sick, using medicines made from plants, and some illnesses were cured this way.

This section of the book looks at prehistoric life all over the world. It begins with the origins of the human race in Africa and how people spread out around the world. It tells how people developed simple tools, survival skills such as hunting and food gathering, and the ability to make clothes and simple shelters. Gradually, human activities such as art, religion and ceremonies developed, signs that social groups were becoming more complex.

Next, we examine the enormous progress made by early peoples, starting with the invention of pottery and the beginnings of farming, which helped men and women control their food supply. Trade then enabled more people to travel and new ideas to spread around the world. The next "revolution" was when people learned how to use metals, by working copper, making bronze and smelting iron. Finally came the invention of writing, the development of large cities and societies, and the end of the prehistoric period. Throughout this period, people overcame tremendous obstacles, such as the huge climate changes of an Ice Age.

▼ WATCHTOWER
*Eventually people
began building
permanent settlements.
The walled city of
Jericho dates from
about 7000BC and is
one of the earliest cities
discovered so far. It had
watchtowers like this
one, which were more
than 9m/30ft high.*

12,000–9000BC	9000–6000BC	6000–4000BC	4000–2000BC	2000BC–AD1
Japanese pot	*Auroch, an early bull*	The climate of what is now the Sahara Desert is very wet. Cattle herding is common in many parts of the region.	*Cuneiform writing from Mesopotamia*	
The dog is domesticated in the Middle East. The first pottery is produced in Japan.	Farming is established in the Fertile Crescent.	Trading towns such as Çatal Hüyük, Turkey, begin to develop.	Potter's wheel invented; bronze-working begins; writing develops. Cities built in Mesopotamia.	
The great ice sheets begin to thaw as temperatures increase. Sea levels rise.	*Clovis points*	Farming spreads to eastern Europe, probably from Turkey.	Stone circles and other megalithic monuments become common in western Europe.	First ironworking transforms tools and weapons.
People in Chile build houses from wood and skins – the first evidence of shelters in the Americas.	The Clovis culture: on the Great Plains people hunt using stone-pointed spears.	*Cotton plant*	The farmers of Mexico domesticate the maize plant. Other crops spread North America.	The Olmec people of Mexico build the region's first large cities.

Finding the Evidence

INDING EVIDENCE ABOUT prehistory is like doing a gigantic jigsaw puzzle with most of the pieces missing. Often very little is now left of the prehistoric peoples who lived thousands of years ago. Archaeologists study every scrap of evidence they can find for clues as to how ancient peoples lived. Sometimes all that remain are a few bits of broken pottery, the foundations of some houses, or the occasional tool or weapon. Archaeologists have to learn what they can from fragments such as these.

Even when there is a big site, a stone circle, for example, or the remains of an ancient town, there are often more questions than answers. What were stone circles used for? Who ruled the first towns? How did people find out how to make bronze? Why did the cave artists paint their pictures? Questions like these still baffle archaeologists. They can suggest answers, but there are no certainties.

Graves can often give archaeologists some of the most fascinating clues about prehistory. They can be almost like time capsules. In many periods, it was the custom to bury a person with some of their possessions. Archaeologists call these items grave goods. These objects can tell us a great deal about the dead person's lifestyle, job and wealth. They can also reveal something about the beliefs of the time. This is because grave goods were usually intended for use in the next world. Such finds suggest that people believed in life after death in prehistoric times. Some of the best evidence, though, comes from the bodies

▲ BURIAL URN
Some prehistoric peoples cremated their dead by burning the bodies on a funeral pyre. The ashes, and sometimes the bones, of the dead person might then be buried in a pottery urn like this one.

◄ CHAMBERED TOMB
This type of tomb, common in prehistoric Europe, often contains several burials. These reveal a lot about ancient society. For example, the grave of a ruler or chief was usually treated differently than the others. It might be more carefully constructed or contain richer goods.

DEATH AND BURIAL
Archaeologists rarely know what they will find when they excavate a grave. There may be only a skeleton, or there may be lavish grave goods as well. Whatever they find, it will probably be very fragile if it has been in the ground for thousands of years.

► GRAVE GOODS
Items in graves often reveal evidence about the spread of technology. For example, these grave goods from a cemetery at Varna in Bulgaria, show that their owners had discovered how to work metal.

◄ TOLLUND MAN
Bodies buried in swamps and bogs are protected from the air. Skin, hair and even clothing can be preserved for hundreds of years. Tollund Man was found buried in a bog in Denmark, and dates from about 210BC.

▲ PASSAGE-GRAVE BURIAL MOUND
Many passage graves dating from around 3,000BC have been found in northern Europe and Ireland. A passage leads to the tomb at the mound's heart.

themselves. By looking at a skeleton, for example, a trained observer can tell roughly how old the person was at their time of death, and whether that person was male or female. It is also possible to measure how tall the dead person was, and to determine quite a lot about build, physical development and strength. Often, archaeologists can find out about a person's diet, by studying the teeth and doing chemical analyses of the bones. Sometimes they can even say why a person died, as some illnesses, such as arthritis, can be detected from the bones.

Studying the features and contents of an ancient grave can provide enough evidence to work out the approximate date when the person was buried. Factors such as the condition of the bones, the way the person was buried, and the type of grave goods that are found with the skeleton, can help to date the burial. How deep the body lies in the ground is also a clue. The deeper it is buried, the older it is likely to be. Archaeologists working in a vertical trench, for example, can often see layers of objects in historical order, from the oldest to the most recent, almost like a timeline.

▶ ARCHAEOLOGICAL DIG
Archaeologists excavate an ancient site. They are working at several different levels. The skeleton is on an earlier level than the remains of the settlement above it. The archaeologists' dig with care, using light tools, such as trowels and brushes, to avoid causing damage. Most importantly of all, they record in detail everything that they find.

Measuring pole

Trowel

Archaeologist drawing remains

Ancient skeleton

Foundations of settlement

Grave goods

▼ EXCAVATING GRAVES
Archaeologists have to be very careful when excavating dead bodies. This is not just because they are delicate. These are remains of real people, and they should be treated with respect. At this grave at Les Eyzies in France, archaeologists have worked slowly to remove the bones, which are at least 10,000 years old.

Dates and Dating

Prehistoric people lived thousands or even millions of years ago. However, because these people left no written records, archaeologists have to rely on other evidence to work out the dates of the remains they find. They have many ways of doing this, from studying the site of the find to using chemical analysis. Even so, nearly all the dates can only be approximate. The older the remains are, the less precise the dates are likely to be.

The abbreviations used with dates in this book are:

- MYA indicates "Million Years Ago". It is used for very ancient dates, a million or more years ago.

- BC indicates the number of years "Before Christ". Jesus Christ lived about 2,000 years ago, so you can work out a "number of years old" by adding 2,000 to a BC date.

The Toolmakers

▲ PEBBLE TOOL
Early hominids chipped away the sides of pebbles to make simple, sharp-edged tools.

PROBABLY THE BIGGEST prehistoric mystery of all is how the human race began. Many scientists think that modern humans evolved, millions of years ago, from creatures that looked rather like apes. They hoped to find a missing link, part-ape and part-human, between modern humans and our animal ancestors. No one has found this missing link. But palaeontologists (people who study fossils, the preserved remains of animals and plants) have discovered the remains of a group of creatures called early hominids. These are animals that share many features with humans. Hominids looked rather ape-like, and had smaller brains than modern humans, but they walked on two legs and could make simple stone tools. Our ancestors were probably rather like ancient hominids.

No one has ever found a complete skeleton of an early hominid. Often all that remains is a fragment of bone or a single tooth. Scientists have tried to find out all about the hominids from such meagre evidence. However, they often disagree about which species of hominid a particular find belongs to, and how the various species relate to each other.

The earliest hominids, which lived in Africa around eight million to one million years ago, are called the australopithecines (meaning southern apes). They stood and walked upright, but were shorter than modern humans, standing 1–1.5m/3–5ft tall. Their bodies had a similar shape to humans, but their flat-nosed faces looked ape-like. Their brains were much smaller than human brains, but larger than those of today's chimpanzees and gorillas.

Australopithecines probably spent most of their time on the ground. Like modern gorillas and chimpanzees, they climbed

◄ PARANTHROPUS ROBUSTUS
Stocky and ape-like, this hominid probably spent some of its time living in trees, but it came down to the ground from time to time to search for food. Like the modern chimpanzee, it probably ate plants most of the time.

HOMO HABILIS
Since Louis Leakey discovered the first specimen of *Homo habilis* in 1964, many similar remains have been found in Africa – especially in the fossil-rich beds of Kenya and Tanzania. Although it is not certain whether these creatures are direct human ancestors, they are definitely our close relatives.

▼ PREDATOR
Early hominids had to guard against fearsome meat-eaters like this sabre-toothed cat. Sometimes the best escape from dangerous animals such as this was to take to the trees.

▲ A LARGER SKULL – A LARGER BRAIN
Homo habilis had a much larger brain than the australopithecines. This was one reason why its discoverers decided that it should be included in the genus *Homo*, just like modern humans. *Homo habilis* lived 2.1 to 1.5 million years ago.

▼ A FIRM GRIP
Homo habilis had a hand that could grip objects firmly. This, together with its brain size, meant that the creature could make simple stone tools and may have been able to build basic shelters from tree branches and leaves.

Pebble tool

Simple brushwood shelter

trees to hide from enemies or to shelter from the rain. Remains of their teeth suggest that they ate mainly plants, plus a little meat. They probably also used the first simple tools.

In 1964, palaeontologist Louis Leakey announced the discovery of the fossilized remains of a previously unknown hominid. It had a larger brain than the southern apes, so Leakey decided to place it in the genus *Homo*, the same as our own species. The fossil was 1.75 million years old, making it our oldest close relative. Stone tools were found near the remains, so Leakey named the fossil *Homo habilis* (handy man).

Like people today, the *Homo habilis* people probably ate quite a lot of meat, but no one knows whether they hunted animals for food or ate the remains left by other animals. Archaeologists have found remains of stone tools next to animal bones, such as simple choppers and hammers made from pebbles. They were probably semi-nomadic, staying in an area for a little while before moving on to a new area for food. When they moved, they left their tools behind.

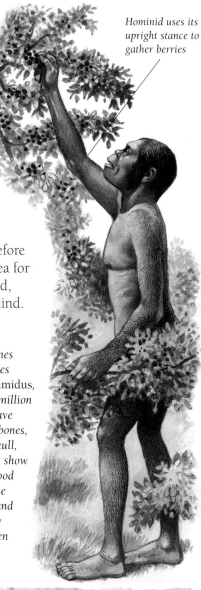

Hominid uses its upright stance to gather berries

▶ "ARDI"
The most complete set of bones from an early hominid species belonged to Ardipithecus ramidus, *which lived more than four million years ago. Archaeologists have nicknamed her "Ardi". The bones, which include most of the skull, teeth, pelvis, hands and feet, show that Ardi was female and stood up to 1.2m/3ft 11in high. She weighed about 50kg/110lb and could walk upright, but may have used all four limbs when moving through trees.*

▲ ROBUSTUS SKULL
The robust australopithecines had heavy skulls with massive jaws and strong ridges of bone across the brows. There were also flanges (areas of bone sticking out from the cheeks) on either side.

▲ AFRICANUS SKULL
Although Australopithecus africanus *had a more lightly built skull than* Paranthropus robustus, *it still had a heavy jaw bone. No one is certain exactly how these two species were related.*

▲ OLDUVAI GORGE
One of the most important hominid sites is Olduvai Gorge in Tanzania, on the Serengeti Plains of East Africa. Fossils of several hominids, including *Homo habilis*, have been found there, making this one of the great hunting grounds in the search for human origins. The gorge contains fossilized remains ranging from 100,000 to around 2 million years old, the older fossils embedded in the deepest rocks. Scatters of tools, from crude pebbles to stone axes, lie near the bones of their makers.

Key Dates

- 7MYA *Sahelanthropus tchadensis* is present in Chad, in Africa. It may be a common ancestor of humans and chimpanzees.

- 4.4MYA *Ardipithecus ramidus* lives in Ethiopia. The most complete early hominid fossil, nicknamed "Ardi", is a member of this species.

- 3.9 to 2.9MYA *Australopithecus afarensis* inhabits East Africa. The most complete example of this species, dubbed "Lucy", was discovered in Hadar, in Ethiopia.

- 2.5MYA Kenya is home to *Paranthropus aethiopicus*, a robust australopithecine.

- 2.1 to 1.5MYA *Homo habilis*, the oldest known member of our genus, exists in Kenya, Tanzania and South Africa.

The Coming of Fire

AROUND 1.6 MILLION YEARS AGO, A GROUP OF hominids mastered a completely new skill. They learned how to use fire, which must have brought about a huge change in their lives. Suddenly, they were able to cook food instead of eating raw meat and plants. They could keep their draughty caves and rock shelters warm in winter. The heat and flames could even be used as weapons against enemies. Fire probably meant that they had a safer and more comfortable life than the earlier hominids had enjoyed.

The hominids who mastered fire were about 1.5m/5ft tall. They had bigger brains and longer limbs than previous hominids, more like those of modern humans. Scientists called them

◀ FIRE STICK
One way early people made fire was to put dry grass on a stick called a hearth. Then they rubbed another stick against the hearth to make a spark and set the grass alight.

FOOD AND RESOURCES

With their larger brains, *Homo erectus* people were probably better at hunting and finding new types of food than previous hominids. Their travels across Africa may have been to search for new sources of food. As well as hunting animals and gathering plants, they probably killed injured animals or scavenged meat left by other predators.

▲ HACKBERRIES
Gathering nuts and fruit, such as these hackberries, provided a large part of the diet of *Homo erectus*. They had to learn by trial and error which berries were good to eat and which were poisonous.

◀ WOOLLY RHINO
The *Homo erectus* people tried eating whatever meat they killed. They may have eaten large creatures like this woolly rhinoceros, hunting them in groups and sharing the meat.

▲ EAST TURKANA
Close to the mountains and lakes of Kenya, the site of East Turkana was one of the first homes of *Homo erectus* around 1.5 million years ago.

Homo erectus (upright man). The *Homo erectus* people were more advanced in other ways. They made better tools than the earlier hominids, and developed a handaxe, a pointed flint tool with two sharp cutting edges. Handaxes were useful for cutting meat, so the *Homo erectus* people could butcher animals more efficiently. As a result, they may have had more incentive to develop their technology, for example creating smaller tools such as cutting blades.

Homo erectus people probably had more advanced social skills than earlier hominids. They may even have developed a simple language which would have enabled them to talk to and cooperate with each other. This meant that they could perform tasks as a group, such as hunting large animals. They may have used fire in their hunting. Some archaeologists think that they lit bush fires to drive large animals into an ambush, where the creatures could be killed by a hunting group.

Fire also meant they could survive in colder

◀ HOMO ERECTUS
Cave-dwelling Homo erectus *people prepare to cook a meal in front of their cave. One member of the group makes stone tools, perhaps to cut up the dead animal, another tends the fire and two children help an adult dismember the carcass before it is cooked on the hot fire.*

climates. This encouraged *Homo erectus* people to travel more widely than earlier hominids. Like *Homo habilis*, they were probably always on the move, making temporary camps as bases for hunting and gathering. Some of these homes may have been seasonal, occupied during the spring or summer when fruit, nuts and leaves were plentiful. But *Homo erectus* people also ventured beyond their native Africa, and were probably the first hominids to settle in Europe and Asia.

▲ ERECTUS SKULL
The skull of Homo erectus *was wider and larger than that of* Homo habilis, *giving room for a larger brain. As the jawbone of* Homo erectus *jutted forwards, this species still had a face that looked more like an ape's than a modern human's.*

◀ EARLY HOMINID SITES, EAST AFRICA
Most of the early remains of *Homo habilis* and *Homo erectus* have come from a cluster of sites in Kenya and Tanzania in East Africa. The structure of the rocks there has helped preserve these fossils. For example, at Olduvai Gorge, hominid bones and tools were left by the shores of a lake, later to be covered by mud and volcanic lava and preserved. Still later, geological faults caused the rocks to move, making the fossils visible.

Sites of
♦ *Homo habilis*
● *Homo erectus*

White Nile
N
● Omo
East Turkana ●● Koobi Fora
R. Congo
L. Victoria
Olduvai ● Gorge
Indian Ocean
L. Tanganyika
AFRICA
L. Nyasa
MADAGASCAR
Zambezi R.
Sterkfontein
Atlantic Ocean
0 — Kilometres — 1500
0 — Miles — 1000

Key Dates

- 2.6MYA The Pleistocene period begins. Animals such as horses, cattle and elephants appear.

- 1.8MYA The earliest *Homo erectus* ever found comes from Georgia, in Eurasia. Variations between skulls found here have led some scientists to suggest that *Homo rudolfensis*, *Homo habilis* and *Homo erectus* are actually all the same species.

- 1.7 to 0.5MYA Some *Homo erectus* (known as Yuanmou Man) have now reached China.

- 1.6MYA *Homo erectus* camp at Chesowanya in the Kenya Rift Valley. This shows possible evidence of the use of fire.

The Spread of Hominids

AROUND 2 MILLION years ago, the world's wildlife was on the move. Many tropical animals started to travel northwards and eastwards. Gradually, they moved away from the sweltering jungles towards cooler parts of the globe. Food was often difficult to find for the early hominids, so the *Homo erectus* people followed the tropical animals to places with more moderate climates. In doing so, they covered great distances, from modern Africa as far as present-day Turkey, India, Sri Lanka, China and Java.

In Europe and Asia, *Homo erectus* people set up camps to which they returned year after year. One of the most famous of all is a series of caves at Zhoukoudien, China. Hominids stayed here for thousands of years (from about 700,000 to about 200,000 years ago), and archaeologists have found the remains of more than 40 *Homo erectus* people at the site. In the caves the archaeologists found a variety of tools, including choppers, scrapers, awls, points and cutters, most of which were made from quartz. The more recent

▲ A PLACE TO SHELTER
At Terra Amata, southern France, there is evidence that hominids made a camp with simple shelters. These small huts were made out of tree branches, weighted down with stones.

in date the tools, the smaller and more finely worked they are. There is also evidence of fire in the Zhoukoudien caves. Similar remains have been found in *Homo erectus* sites in Europe and South-east Asia. They reveal a people who gathered leaves and berries, but were also cunning enough to hunt large mammals. The people moved around from one season to the next. If they could not find caves, they built simple shelters from branches and stones. They probably wrapped animal skins around themselves to keep warm in the winter.

One mystery is that many surviving *Homo erectus* skulls have had their bases removed. Some scientists think that this was done so that survivors could take out the brain. Perhaps these people were the first cannibals? There may be other reasons, such as to make containers to carry water.

Another puzzle is how *Homo erectus* died out. There are no *erectus* remains later than about 200,000 years ago. It is not known whether they perished because other hominids killed them, because their food supplies ran out, or because of ill health.

ANCIENT CULTURE

The *Homo erectus* people were able to produce a wider variety of tools, weapons and other items than the earlier hominids, although the only objects to survive in large numbers are their stone tools. They were skilled flintworkers, creating implements with razor-sharp edges for butchering meat, cutting plant food and scraping hides. They were probably also woodworkers, using wood to build simple shelters and make weapons such as spears and clubs.

▶ PAINT
Stones marked with red ochre, a natural earth pigment, have been found at Becov in Bohemia, Europe. These finds date to 250,000 years ago, and suggest that people may have decorated their bodies or items that they made. They may have mixed the ochre with fat to make a form of paint.

◀ UPRIGHT MAN
Homo erectus people looked very like modern humans, except for their ape-like faces. But they were not as tall as most people today.

◀ HANDAXE
The double-edged stone tool was *Homo erectus*' most common and useful implement. It fitted comfortably into the hand, and was easy to carry around. The two sharp edges could be used for cutting or chopping.

▼ ON THE HUNT

A group of Homo erectus *people have worked together to trap three elephants in a swamp. They are now about to move in on one of the animals, to attack it with wooden spears and clubs.*

Swampy ground

Wooden spear

Wooden club

▲ HOMO ERECTUS SITES

This successful hominid spread from Africa to both Asia and Europe. As well as sites in China, there are also many places in Europe with early hominid remains. In the case of most of the European sites, experts are uncertain whether the occupants were *Homo erectus* or an early form of our own species.

Key Dates

- 1.5MYA *Homo erectus* has reached Ubeidiya, by the Jordan and Yarmuk Rivers, Israel.

- 1.2MYA *Homo erectus* living in Olduvai Gorge, Tanzania.

- 1.1MYA *Homo erectus* settles in Europe.

- 1 to 0.7MYA *Homo erectus* is present in central Java. The hominids' long-distance movements show them adapting to different environments.

- 700,000–200,000BC *Homo erectus* living at Zhoukoudien Cave, near Beijing, China.

Neanderthals

▲ CAVE WOMAN
Neanderthals like this female may have been the first hominids to care for the sick and disabled. This prolonged the lives of individuals who would otherwise have met painful early deaths.

A TYPICAL CAVE MAN IS usually portrayed as a stocky creature with heavy bones, a thick ridge across the brows and a blank expression on his face. As far as we can tell, the Neanderthals, who lived in Europe and the Middle East 70,000 to 35,000 years ago, did look rather like this. They are our closest relatives among the hominids, and were intelligent with brains a similar size to our own. In fact, the Neanderthals were so similar to modern humans that some scientists place them in our own species, giving them a sub-species (*Homo sapiens neanderthalensis*). Others give them a species of their own (*Homo neanderthalensis*).

The Neanderthal people used their intelligence to develop tools and technology. Although their tools were still made of stone, they now had specialized items such as chisels and borers. They made these tools by chipping small flakes off carefully selected cores, or lumps, of flint. To chip off a flake of the right size and sharpness, a Neanderthal flintworker needed skill, patience and a very great deal of practice.

Some of the most fascinating evidence about the Neanderthals comes from their burial sites. Several of these have been discovered, from the Dordogne, France, to the Zagros Mountains in Iran. They reveal the bodies placed carefully in their graves. Items such as animal horns or bones were deliberately placed around them, probably as part of a burial ritual. Sites like these have led modern archaeologists to believe that the Neanderthals were the first hominids to develop burial ceremonies. The burial sites also provided a great deal of evidence that enabled scientists to work out what these people looked like, from

Neanderthal   Modern human

◀ SKELETONS
Stockily built and with a large head, Neanderthals were strong hominids with brains about as big as our own. Modern humans were taller and more upright.

NEANDERTHAL LIFE
During much of the Neanderthals' lifetime, Europe and Asia were in the grip of an ice age. The Neanderthals had to adapt to the cold, making clothes from skins and finding whatever shelter they could. This necessity, together with their large brains, made them inventive and adaptable.

chopper

scraper

borer

◀ NEANDERTHAL TOOLS
The Neanderthals developed different tools for scraping, cutting, butchering and boring holes in hides. These flint-working skills have been perfected over many generations.

◀ POLLEN GRAINS
By examining prehistoric pollen under a microscope, scientists have found that trees such as alder, birch, oak and elm grew in areas in which the Neanderthals lived.

▲ NEANDERTHAL GRAVE
Skeletons from this grave at La Chapelle-aux-Saints in France, were found to be deformed and stooping. This could mean the people suffered from arthritis.

Flower offerings

Bone offerings

Animal horns

◀ BURIAL
A group of Neanderthals bury one of their dead. As mourners look on, two members of the group make offerings of pollen and flowers, which are placed carefully on and around the deceased's body. Animal horns are positioned to mark the grave. Rituals like this are the earliest known ceremonies.

their stocky build to the size of their heads and brains.

Some of the skeletons showed signs of bone diseases, such as arthritis, that must have developed over many years. Any individual who developed such a disease would not have been able to hunt and gather food. Other members of their family group must have fed them and looked after them. So as well as being intelligent, the Neanderthals may have been the first carers, helping relatives who were not able to fend for themselves. The Neanderthals died out around 35,000 years ago, but it is not certain why. They may have perished through disease, or have been killed by Cro-Magnons, *Homo sapiens* who lived at the same time. New evidence is now being found to suggest that Neanderthals interbred with Cro-Magnon people.

Key Dates

- 120,000BC Neanderthals living from Europe to Mesopotamia.

- 100,000–40,000BC Neanderthals develop stone tools for several different purposes.

- 100,000BC Neanderthals and *Homo sapiens* both living at Qafzeh, Israel.

- 50,000BC Remains of a burial site of this date found at Shanidar Cave, northern Iraq.

- 40,000BC Skull of this date found at Monte Circeo, Italy, had been smashed to remove the brain.

- 35,000BC Neanderthals die out.

▲ NEANDERTHAL SITES
The homeland of the Neanderthals stretched from France and Germany to Mesopotamia in the east. The eastern and western populations were separated during ice ages, but both groups produced similar tools and buried their dead in a similar way.

Wise Man

▲ FIRE
The discovery of fire by Homo erectus *was an enormous technological advance that* Homo sapiens *would have inherited.*

B
Y THE TIME OF THE Neanderthals, members of our own species, *Homo sapiens*, or "wise man" were also living in many parts of the world. In some places, Neanderthals and humans lived close together, which suggests that Neanderthals could not have been our direct ancestors. If they lived together, we could not have evolved from both species. If this is correct, who were they?

Homo sapiens may have evolved from *Homo erectus*, or from another similar hominid that has not yet been discovered. Hominid bones, found in sites all over the world, seem to share features of *Homo erectus* and *Homo sapiens*. Although similar in size to ourselves, these hominids have bone ridges above the eyes and flattened skulls rather than dome-like heads. They mostly date from around 150,000 to 120,000 years ago and are classified by archaeologists as archaic *Homo sapiens*.

Some remains of *Homo sapiens* date from not long after these "archaic" bones.

◀ HUMAN FORM
The first members of Homo sapiens *were similar in appearance to modern people, except that they were generally rather shorter in height. Their upright build made them well adapted to walking on two legs.*

▶ COUNTING STICK
Lengths of bone with small notches cut into them have been found at some Homo sapiens *sites. These may have been counting devices, or an early form of writing. They may have been used to record a person's share of food.*

◀ EARLY HUMAN SKULL
Early humans had broad skulls that contained large brains. Their faces were flat, so they did not have the ape-like appearance of hominids like Homo habilis *or the Neanderthals.*

THE EARLY HUNTERS
The search for food was the most important part of life for early *Homo sapiens*. Some groups hunted herds of antelopes on the grasslands. Others went into the hills after wild sheep and goats, or to the coast in search of seals and seafood.

◀ SEALS
For northern people who lived near the sea, such animals as seals were a valuable quarry. The animals provided a supply of meat, skins, bones (for tool-making) and blubber.

▲ BONE CARVING
Among the hominids, humans are the only artists. Early hunters liked to carve the creatures they chased, and animal bone was an ideal material – soft enough to carve but hard enough to last.

▲ SKULL, QAFZEH, ISRAEL
This is one of several skulls that have puzzled archaeologists. Experts are not sure if it is a Neanderthal or human. The latest tests suggest that the two species lived together and bred, so specimens like this may have had a parent from each species.

Some experts think humans evolved in one area of Africa and then spread gradually across the world. This idea, which archaeologists refer to as the "Out of Africa" theory is backed up by research based on DNA. This is the chemical in *Homo sapiens* bodies containing genes.

Other scientists believe that modern humans evolved separately in different parts of the world. For example, the population in South-east Asia could have descended from *Homo erectus* people on Java. Europeans could have evolved from hominids from the Middle East that had interbred with Neanderthals.

By 100,000 to 90,000 years ago, modern humans had evolved in southern and eastern Africa. From here they moved northwards, crossing the Sahara and reaching the Middle East. For thousands of years the Sahara was wetter than it is today, and it was covered with grasslands cropped by grazing mammals.

Hominids could cross this green Sahara with ease. By 75,000 years ago there were modern humans in eastern Asia. Later still, they would reach and settle in Europe.

As our ancestors spread across the globe, they settled in many different environments, from the warm African grasslands to the cold forests of northern Europe. They used their skills to adapt to each new place, using local materials to make clothes and huts, finding out about plants and animals, and learning how to fish. These early people were highly advanced compared to many species.

▶ PREPARING SKINS
A hunted animal was not just a source of meat. The skins of larger creatures were removed, scraped clean, and trimmed. Then they were made into clothes, coverings for shelters, and simple bags and containers.

◀ EARLY HUMAN SITES
By 35,000 years ago, early humans had spread across most of Africa. They developed different lifestyles and tools to cope with the different conditions and materials that they found. The people of northern Africa, for example, produced quite finely worked flint scrapers and handaxes, similar to those made by the Neanderthals in Europe. In the south, however, many of the tools were much less finely chipped stone points and scrapers, but they were still sharp and effective.

Key Dates

- 150,000–120,000BC Archaic *Homo sapiens*, the most ancient form of our own species, appears.

- 100,000BC Modern humans begin to evolve in Africa.

- 100,000–70,000BC African sites south of the Sahara show signs of modern human occupation. *Homo erectus* is still alive, but is slowly replaced by *Homo sapiens*.

- 100,000–40,000BC The Sahara is cooler than today. Hominids cross it to reach northern Africa.

- 75,000BC Ice sheets in the northern hemisphere begin to get larger.

The First Europeans

▲ BISON CAVE PAINTING
When they discovered how to make pigments out of earth and minerals, people began to paint pictures like this bison.

LIFE WAS HARD FOR THE first humans who lived in Europe. The climate was colder than it is today. Food could be difficult to find and dangerous animals lurked in the forests. People survived by adapting, and by becoming skilled at making things, such as tools and shelters. Slowly, over many thousands of years, they perfected the essential skills for survival.

The early Europeans are often called Cro-Magnons, after a site in the Dordogne, France. Cro-Magnon people kept themselves warm by making clothes from animal skins. They sheltered in caves when they could, but natural shelter was not always easy to find. They learned how to make simple homes, using whatever materials they could find. Tree branches provided a framework, and was covered with turf or animal skins to keep out the wind and rain. Another solution was to make a framework from the massive bones of woolly mammoths they had killed.

The Cro-Magnons were skilled toolmakers. Their best and sharpest tools were made from flint, which they could work into small points for spearheads and knives. They also used materials such as bone and deer antler to make tools. Small pieces of bone could be carved to make pointed needles, and antlers could be adapted to make tools such as hammers.

Wood was another useful material. Small flakes of flint could be wedged into a twig to make a knife with a handle. The shafts of spears were also made of wood. It is likely that wood was used in many other ways too, such as making simple containers, but all evidence of this has perished with time.

The greatest achievement of the early European people was in their art. It ranged from sculpture to cave painting and tells us a great deal about everyday life. Pictures of

◀ KALEMBA ROCK SHELTER
About 35,000 years ago, hunter-gatherers used this natural shelter at Kalemba in Zambia. Like other similar shelters all over Africa, it provided a good resting place for people out hunting animals or searching for plants to eat.

GROWING SKILLS

The remains and tools of early *Homo sapiens* seem primitive, but early humans were in fact very intelligent. They were using their abilities to adapt to all sorts of different environments. Human language must also have been developing during this period, but unfortunately no record of it exists.

◀ BEZOAR GOAT
This species of goat was a popular quarry for hunters in the rocky, mountainous regions of the Middle East. Groups of hunters would drive a herd into a canyon. Then they could kill as many as they needed and share out the meat between a large number of people.

flint knife

antler hammer

stone spearhead

bone knives

▲ TOOLS
People learned to use several different materials to make tools. If no good stone was available, people used bone and antler for knives and points, as well as for tools like hammers.

◀ HUNTERS' CAMP
Early hunters covered quite long distances looking for food, but returned to regular camps at places where there was shelter and a water supply. A campsite could be used by members of the same tribe or group for thousands of years.

animals show the creatures they hunted, from woolly mammoths and rhinoceroses to wild oxen and deer. It is also possible to make out the skin clothing they wore. Female figurines suggest that the people worshipped a mother goddess or goddess of fertility. People who were intelligent enough to produce the art and tools of the early Europeans probably also had quite an advanced society. Although they lived in family-based bands, it is quite likely that these small groups may have come together at certain times. They probably joined together to hunt, or for religious ceremonies celebrating important times of the year.

Australopithecus   Homo erectus   Homo sapiens

▲ THE GROWING BRAIN
Studies of early *Homo sapiens* show that their brains were similar in size to those of modern humans, and much bigger than those of the earlier hominids. The australopithecines, which were the size of modern chimpanzees, had brains with an average cubic capacity just over half that of *Homo erectus*. Even the brain of *Homo erectus* was little over half the total volume of *Homo sapiens'* brain. Human inventiveness, creativity, language and social skills are all the result of our bigger brains.

Key Dates

- 43,000BC *Homo sapiens* established in Bulgaria.

- 40,000BC Humans in western Europe living alongside Neanderthals.

- 35,000BC The Neanderthals die out. *Homo sapiens* is the only human form in Europe.

- 20,000BC French and Spanish flint-workers find out how to bake flints so they can be pressure flaked to make very fine shapes.

- 16,000–12,000BC Human settlement in Russia and Siberia. Mammoth-bone huts built at Mezhrich.

- 6000BC Europeans develop microliths, tools made of tiny fragments of flint.

The Ice Age

THE EARTH'S WEATHER IS ALWAYS changing. For the last two million years, the temperature of the planet has see-sawed up and down. This has produced a series of warm periods with cold ice ages in between. The last of these ice ages reached its peak about 18,000BC. The time around this peak (30,000 to 12,000BC) is so important in human history that it is always known as the Ice Age.

Humans had spread over much of the world by the beginning of the most recent Ice Age. All that time, the ice sheets had pushed down from the north, covering huge areas of the globe. Places such as Scandinavia, Siberia and northern Britain, became unfit for humans.

During this period, much of northern Europe was covered with sparse tundra. Large parts of Spain, Greece and the Balkans covered in forests. The area north of the Black Sea in Russia was a vast grassland. These varied habitats were a challenge to early people, and they had to adapt to different conditions. Big-game hunters moved across the Russian plains. Hunter-fishers lived on the tundra and at the edge of the ice sheets. Hunters and food gatherers took shelter in the forests. People had to devise different tools, hunting techniques and social skills to suit these varied lifestyles.

Ice Age tools are more varied than those of previous peoples. People in the Ice Age still used stone for their knives and choppers. But they used more bone and

▲ CARVING
This head is carved from a piece of mammoth tusk, a material often used for sculpture during the Ice Age.

◀ MAMMOTH
This large Ice Age mammal ranged widely across Europe, Asia and North America. It died out around 10,000 years ago.

ICE AGE LIFE

The Ice Age made life difficult in many places. The cold was not just uncomfortable, it meant that some food plants could not survive. In addition, many areas had few or no trees, meaning that people had no wood to make shelters. These difficulties forced people to find new ways of life. They had to experiment with new foods (such as fish) and new materials (such as, bones and antlers).

▼ MAKING FIRE
In a cold, damp climate, fire became even more important as a source of warmth. Making fire by rubbing sticks together to create a spark may have spread across Europe during the Ice Age.

◀ REINDEER
There are many surviving tools, harpoons and carvings made from antler. This shows that reindeer-like animals were hunted across Europe during the Ice Age. Reindeer provided tasty, nutritious meat, as well as hides, bone and antler.

▲ HARPOON POINTS
Ice Age hunters used harpoons for killing animals such as seals and for fishing in the rivers for salmon. The points took a long time to carve from deer antler and were prized possessions.

▶ MAMMOTH HUNTING
Large, fierce and with two powerful tusks, woolly mammoths were
an awesome sight for the people of the Ice Age. But these dangerous
creatures were such a good source of meat, skins, bones and ivory
that the people risked injury or even death hunting and trapping them.

antler than before. They discovered how to use antler to make strong handles for stone blades and axeheads. They carved bone to make needles, which were essential to sew together hides and furs for warm clothes.

People still hunted large mammals such as the woolly mammoth. They also learned how to track and hunt animals that live in herds, such as reindeer. This gave them a rich source of hides, meat and antlers.

Because resources were scarce, Ice Age people probably became the first traders, swapping food and materials. Flints and furs, for example, could be traded for food in times of shortage. People moved about more, they met other groups and they probably found out about new sources of food. Contact with other tribes was an aid to survival. When different groups met it became necessary to have a leader to act as spokesman. This was also a time when personal adornment first became important. A bone pendant or bright body paint could mark out the leader of a group.

▲ ICE AGE WORLD
Lower sea levels meant that the world's continents were larger during the Ice Age, and some landmasses that are now separate were joined together. But the ice sheets in Europe, Asia and the Americas made vast areas of this land unfit for human life.

Key Dates

- 32,000–28,000BC Aurignacian culture in western Europe produces flint scrapers and sharpened blades.

- 30,000–12,000BC Main period of last Ice Age.

- 24,000BC Hunter-gatherers in Europe build permanent dwellings.

- 20,000BC Hunters in western Europe develop spears and spear-throwers. Hunters in Poland use mammoth-tusk boomerangs.

- 18,000BC Peak of Ice Age.

- 18,000–12,500BC People settled near Kebara Cave, Israel, make grinding stones. This suggests they were gathering and processing grains.

Images of the Ice Age

▲ MAMMOTH CARVING
Ice Age art was not always realistic, and carvers often made striking, stylized shapes. In the case of this mammoth, the shape of the animal reflects the shape of the bone from which it is carved.

THE PREHISTORIC CAVE paintings of Europe show a wide variety of creatures. These include groups of wild horses, herds of reindeer and wild oxen, wild cats, birds and mammoths. The animals are shown in action, galloping and running across the cave walls as if they are being chased by human hunters. They are dramatic action pictures, yet they were produced in dark, damp conditions in chilly caves.

Ice Age artists also made sculptures and figures from clay. They engraved cave walls and carved antlers and mammoth tusks into models of animals.

The paintings and sculptures are often hidden so deep in underground caverns that many of them were not rediscovered until the 1900s. It is not known why the paintings were hidden away like this. In fact, no one really knows why the pictures were produced at all. Most experts agree that there was probably some religious reason for the

paintings. They may have been used in magic ceremonies designed to help hunters, or to promote fertility. Sometimes there are several different outlines in the same place, one drawn over another. This makes some cave paintings and engravings very difficult to see. Experts have spent many hours redrawing them in

▲ PAINTING TECHNIQUES
Artists used brushes or pads of animal hair when painting on cave walls. They sometimes put on the paint with their fingers, or created a bold outline by drawing with charcoal.

ICE AGE ART

Because we do not know why Ice Age artists made their pictures and sculptures, it is difficult to decide what their work means. It does show how important animals and the natural world were to them. The cave paintings show the kind of animals these people hunted and ate, and also which creatures they thought were the most powerful. These images, and the small carvings of the time, also provide some clues about Ice Age beliefs.

◀ ANTLER SPEAR-THROWER
A spear-thrower helped a hunter hurl his spear faster and farther than he could unaided by acting as an extension of his arm. This made it easier to kill swift creatures such as deer. Hunters prized their spear-throwers, which were usually made of antler. This material lent itself to carving, and spear-throwers are often beautifully decorated. Swift-running animals like the horse shown here were popular subjects.

◀ VENUS FIGURINE
Carvings of female figures, with their hips and bellies enlarged, have often been found at Ice Age sites. Archaeologists think they are fertility goddesses, and so have named them "Venus" figures, after the Roman goddess of love.

▶ IVORY HEAD
This female head from France, carved in ivory, shows a goddess. Goddess figures have been found in most areas of Europe, from France to Russia, so goddesses were probably the most important deities in Ice Age religion.

their notebooks to try to make the outlines clearer. For the prehistoric artist, the act of making the image seems to have been more important than the finished result. Perhaps the actual process of painting or engraving was part of a religious ceremony.

Ice Age painters used chalk to make white, charcoal for black, ochre, a kind of earth, for yellow, and iron oxide for red. Sometimes artists used minerals that they could heat to make other pigments. These were mixed with water and applied with fur pads, animal-hair brushes or just with the artist's fingers.

Another technique involved spitting the paint out of the mouth or a reed to make a simple spray effect. The artists used oil lamps to light the caves and sometimes built crude wooden frameworks to gain extra height while working. With these simple techniques, Ice Age artists produced images that were surprisingly complex for such a simple society.

▲ CAVE PAINTING, LASCAUX
The caves at Lascaux, France, contain perhaps the most brilliant of all the known prehistoric paintings. Discovered in 1940, they show a variety of animals, including reindeer and horses. These finely drawn, bright paintings began to show signs of damage during the 1960s because the atmosphere in the caves was affected by so many visitors. The caves were closed to the public, who now visit a replica called Lascaux II.

◀ ANTELOPE
This painting from a cave at Font de Gaume, France, shows the skill of the ancient artists. They caught the outline of the creature's head and horns, and cleverly shaded the animal's hide to create a sense of its bulk.

▶ MAKING PAINT
Artists found their pigments in the earth and rocks. They mixed soils and minerals that they found with a medium such as water or animal fat. This produced a type of spreadable paint. They could also draw directly on to the rock surface with pieces of charcoal (burnt wood) or chalk.

iron oxide

brushstrokes   *chalk*   *charcoal*

◀ LAMP
Many cave paintings are hidden in dark, underground caverns. The artists needed light to see what they were doing, so they used fires, flaming torches or stone lamps like this one. The animal fat was burnt in the lamps, to give a bright, but rather smelly, flame. Several hundred Ice Age lamps have been found by archaeologists.

Key Dates

- 30,000BC Earliest European cave art.

- 30,000BC European musicians make flutes from lengths of animal bone.

- 23,000BC First cave paintings made in the Dordogne, France.

- 23,000BC Venus figurines made in France and central Europe.

- 18,000–8000BC Main period of cave painting in caves at Lascaux, France, and Altamira, Spain.

- 16,000BC Antler and bone carving reaches its peak. Finely engraved and carved spear points and spear-throwers made.

- 11,000BC Cave painting ends.

The First Australians

▲ ENGRAVINGS
These patterns were cut into rocks at Panaramitee, Australia, thousands of years ago. They may be the world's oldest rock engravings.

DURING THE ICE AGE, the sea level was much lower than it is today. The channels separating Australia from islands such as Timor in Indonesia were far narrower. As a result, groups of islanders took to the sea in bamboo rafts or simple boats in search of fish and shellfish. Some time before 32,000 years ago some Indonesians found themselves on the coast of what is now Australia. No one knows whether they deliberately looked for new land, or whether they were blown off-course on one of their fishing trips. They moved inland and became the first humans to inhabit the Australian continent.

The remains of early settlement in Australia are quite patchy. The

▶ DUG-OUT CANOE
Early sailors, like the people who first crossed from South-east Asia to Australia, may have hollowed out and smoothed wooden logs to make simple dug-out canoes.

people were spread over a wide area and must have covered vast distances both by sea and on foot. Stone tools, hearths, shell debris, fish bones and other remnants point to a scattered population between 32,000 and 24,000 years ago. Important sites include Devil's Lair Cave near Perth, Western Australia, a rock shelter near the Cleland Hills in Northern Territory and Koonalda Cave in South Australia.

At Devil's Lair, archaeologists found several items that were probably used in religious ceremonies. There were some stone plaques and a pit with human teeth that had been removed by sharp blows. At Koonalda Cave, the inhabitants engraved lines on the rock walls. Native Australians carried on making rock engravings into the 1900s. The finds dating from prehistoric times show how far back a rich native Australian culture goes.

Many early Australian sites were occupied for thousands of years. This can also make exact dating

A SCATTERED PEOPLE

The first Australians walked vast distances across their country to find food and good campsites. When they settled, they spread out thinly across the country. Sites in the south, which were well away from their original landing places, seem to have been most popular. The settlement process probably took place very slowly, spreading across the country over thousands of years.

◀ NECKLACE
People wore necklaces made of shells and animal teeth. Ornamentation like this may have been a sign that the wearer was an important person. Such necklaces have been found in Asia as well as Australia. This indicates that the two regions were linked by a common people.

◀ HAND STENCILS
Stencils like this were probably made by spitting paint around and over the artist's hand. This type of art has been produced in Australia since at least 22,000BC. The images, which are on the walls of rock shelters in southern and eastern Australia, show the importance of art to the island continent's earliest people.

of the art and artefacts difficult for archaeologists. One rock shelter, at Puritjarra, was used for nearly 7,000 years.

People had reached the island of Tasmania at the south-east tip of Australia by 32,000 years ago. They remained there even when the final Ice Age was at its coldest, when much of the island was covered by tundra and grassland. They lived in caves and rock shelters, and survived by hunting the local animals, mainly the kangaroo and the wallaby. The new Tasmanians developed their own style of art. They painted hand stencils on cave walls, and made tools

from a natural form of glass that they discovered in a crater formed by a meteorite from space.

The native people of Australia developed a lifestyle long ago that has lasted in some places to the present day. Over the millenia they adapted as their environment changed, from the chill Ice Age to the hot, dry climate of today.

▼ MAKING TOOLS
Early Australians became expert stoneworkers. They could chip away stones to make tools that were the right shape for the job and grind the edges of tools such as axes to make them sharp. Some of their tools were traded over long distances.

◄ EXPLORERS' MAP
Because the sea level was lower, larger pieces of land were above water, so the first people to travel to Australia had a shorter sea journey than navigators would have to make today. They probably crossed from places such as Java or the Celebes, sailing from island to island until they reached the north-western coast of Australia. Even for such short trips, they needed to be good sailors and navigators. They probably built up their sailing skills over many years fishing off the South-east Asian coasts.

Key Dates

- 30,000BC Human settlement of Australia probably begins.

- 29,000BC People are living in Tasmania, which is linked to the Australian mainland by a land bridge.

- 25,000BC Puritjarra Rock Shelter, near the Cleland Hills, Northern Territory, is occupied.

- 24,000BC Signs of human occupation near Lake Mungo, New South Wales.

- 22,000BC Traces of human settlement at Koonalda Cave, on the Nullaboor Plain, South Australia.

- 10,000BC The population of native Australians is about 300,000 people.

Early Americans

THE FIRST AMERICANS probably came from the extreme north tip of Asia, which is now Siberia. In the Ice Age the two continents were connected by a land bridge. The first peoples to cross this narrow neck of land found themselves in North America's bleakest, coldest spot. There would have been little vegetation. Most of their food came from hunting and fishing. They were well prepared for this, because the climate in Siberia was similar to that in North America. Many moved south in search of better weather and more plentiful food.

Archaeologists disagree about exactly when the first Americans arrived. The earliest firm evidence of

▲ THE JOURNEY FROM SIBERIA
It was a long, hard journey from Siberia across the land bridge to North America. We do not know what made people start this journey, but perhaps the harsh Ice Age conditions made them want to look for a place where food, warmth and comfort were easier to find.

humans dates to between 15,000 and 12,000 years ago. However, in the same period, there is more widespread evidence for a hunting people who lived in central North America. Archeologists called them the

THE GREAT MIGRATION
How do we know that the first Americans came from Siberia? One clue lies in the way the early Americans made tools and weapons. Many chipped tiny flint blades from bigger lumps of stone. They jammed these flints into grooves along the edge of a piece of bone to make a spearhead. Spearheads with this design have been found in both Siberia and North America.

▼ MAMMOTH TUSKS
These fossilized tusks are among many mammoth remains preserved at the Hot Springs mammoth site, South Dakota. They show that the first American hunters were catching the same quarry as their ancestors in Asia.

▲ WEAVING
A few fragments of twine have survived at Guitarrero Cave, Peru, to show that people could weave 10,000 years ago. These pieces may have been part of a bag or similar container.

▲ CLOVIS POINTS
North American mammoth hunters fitted these finely worked sharp stone points to their spears. They made these points out of several different types of stone.

Clovis people. They left behind finely worked flint spearheads, now called Clovis points after the city where the tools were found. These have been found at several places near the bones of large mammals such as mammoth and bison, particularly in Arizona and New Mexico. Clovis people probably hunted solitary animals, driving them into swamps where they could be killed.

As the ice melted, the large mammals became extinct, although no one really knows why. The Clovis people vanished as a variety of new environments, from vast woodlands to arid deserts, developed in North America. People learned to adapt to each environment, evolving into distinct societies, whose lifestyles changed little until recent centuries.

In South America there is also evidence for human settlement by 12,000 years ago. At Monte Verde, Chile, the cremated remains of humans have been found in a cave. This site also contains remains of two rows of huts with wooden frames that supported a covering of animal skins. The huts had clay-lined pits for cooking and there were larger, communal hearths outside.

It is just possible that human life began in South America much earlier than the

▶ MONTE VERDE
The huts at Monte Verde, Chile, made of wood covered with skins, provide the earliest evidence in America for man-made shelters. The remains were preserved in peaty soil, along with items such as a wooden bowl and digging sticks.

◀ SPEARHEAD
Spears, with notched bone spearheads bound tightly to wooden shafts with animal sinews, were used by early American hunters.

huts at Monte Verde. At Pedra Furada Rock Shelter, Brazil, there are areas of painted rock which some scientists date to around 32,000 years ago. Not all authorities agree with this dating, or with similar dates for some of the stone tools found at Monte Verde. If the early dates are correct, it is likely that settlement also began much earlier in North America, but that the people left no surviving remains.

◀ NEW ARRIVALS
The first North Americans worked their way between the two main ice sheets. The Bering Land Bridge was created between Siberia and Alaska because the sea level was some 100m/300ft lower than it is today. Some people may also have come along the west coast on boats or rafts, stopping every so often along the edge of the Cordilleran Ice Sheet. When they finally reached beyond the ice, they found a vast empty land. Some people quickly moved east and west, while others pushed on further south.

Key Dates

- 13,000BC Hunters from Siberia cross the Bering Land Bridge.

- 12,500BC Humans at Meadowcroft Rock Shelter, Pittsburgh, Pennsylvania – the earliest known settlement in North America.

- 11,000BC People living at Monte Verde in southern Chile.

- 9000BC Clovis people hunting on the Great Plains.

- 8000BC Human settlers are accompanied by dogs.

- 7500BC The people of the Sloan site, Arkansas, bury their dead. This cemetery is the earliest discovered in North America.

The Thaw Begins

▲ FISH CARVING
Stone carvings of fishes, like this one, were found at Lepenski Vir on the River Danube. They may have portrayed a fish god.

At the end of the Ice Age there was a massive change in the world's climate. In much of Europe, Asia and North America, the ice melted, making the sea level rise and causing floods in flat areas near the sea. The land bridge between Siberia and Alaska disappeared, cutting off North America from Asia. Britain, which had been joined to Europe, was now cut off by the North Sea. Large areas of land were lost around the coasts of Denmark and Sweden.

The change must have been terrifying at first. Many people fled the floods to settle in new areas. Their way of life changed. At the same time, the warmer weather transformed the landscape. In many places, ice and tundra were

▶ THATCHED TENTS
The Middle Stone Age settlement of Lepenski Vir was home to around 100 hunting and fishing people. They lived in tent-like houses made of wooden poles which were probably covered with thatch.

replaced by thick woods of birch and mixed forests in northern Europe, and deciduous woods in the south. People soon realized that these changes gave them new types of food. Among the woods lived animals such as wild pig and deer. Near the coast there were seals, waterfowl and, in many places, shellfish. Food was more plentiful because the climate was warmer.

People developed new methods of hunting and fishing. These new techniques were more efficient than previous methods, so they did not have to move around so much to hunt for food. They set up special camps where food of a certain type was plentiful, or where they could mine flint to make their tools and weapons.

Most settlements in this period were by rivers or near the sea, where the people could usually rely on a good food supply. Rivers and coastal waters were the highways of the Stone Age. Rivers provided a way to get through the dense forests. People paddled along in their dug-out canoes, perhaps exchanging valuable goods, such as furs or flint tools, with other people they met along the way.

LIFE DURING THE THAW

As the ice melted, some people moved inland, but for many the sea was too useful to leave behind. Such shellfish as oysters and whelks supplied tasty, nourishing food, so many people returned to the coast for at least part of the year.

scrapers, blades and points from Star Carr

▲ FOREST FRUITS
The trees and shrubs of the new woodlands and forest edges yielded fruits such as blackberries to feed European gatherers.

▲ WILD BOAR
This woodland animals thrived in Europe after the thaw. It became a preferred target for many European hunters.

▲ TOOLS FROM STAR CARR
Hunter-gatherers camped regularly at Star Carr, near a lake in Yorkshire, England, at the end of the final Ice Age. They left behind many stone tools, such as scrapers, which they must have used to prepare animal skins, and smaller sharp cutting blades for butchering meat.

The new lifestyle meant that the people who lived in Europe after the Ice Age were on the whole better fed and more comfortable than their ancestors. They were more settled, so they had time to develop more advanced toolmaking skills. This made them more successful still. As a result, many more of their children began to survive to become adults. The total number of people began to rise and the population began to spread, finding better places to settle and new sources of food.

▼ PINCEVANT
These round tents, held up with wooden poles, were the summer homes of people at Pincevant, France, at the end of the final Ice Age. All that was left to show modern archaeologists that tents had been pitched there were the rings of stones that had held the edges in place, together with hearths and some animal bones.

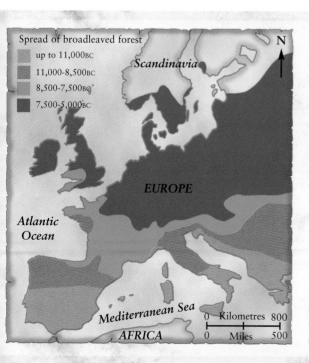

◀ SPREADING FORESTS
As the ice melted, forests spread slowly across Europe, covering the area in broadleaved trees. The spread of the forests began in the south, working its way north over a period of about 6000 years towards Poland and Scandinavia, where mixed conifer and broadleaved forests grew. This new pattern of forests and woodland provided large areas of Europe with their typical landscape, one which survived for thousands of years. It still survives in some parts of Germany, central Europe and Scandinavia.

Map legend:
Spread of broadleaved forest
- up to 11,000 BC
- 11,000–8,500 BC
- 8,500–7,500 BC
- 7,500–5,000 BC

Scandinavia
EUROPE
Atlantic Ocean
Mediterranean Sea
AFRICA

N

0 — Kilometres — 800
0 — Miles — 500

Key Dates

- 13,000 BC The ice thaws, sea levels rise and lowland areas flood.

- 11,000 BC The dog is domesticated in the Middle East.

- 8000 BC Temperatures reach roughly their present levels in Europe.

- 8000 BC The Mesolithic period, or Middle Stone Age, begins in Europe.

- 7500 BC Red deer hunters settle at Star Carr, Yorkshire, England.

- 6500 BC Britain is cut off from Europe.

- 5500 BC Denmark is cut off from the rest of Scandinavia.

- 5000 BC Deciduous forests cover much of Europe.

A Better Food Supply

▲ MATTOCK HEAD
Deer antler was a good material to make a heavy tool such as a mattock. This was used by gatherers for loosening soil and cutting away plant roots for food.

MANY THINGS CHANGED IN North America at the end of the Ice Age. People were suddenly much freer to go where they wanted in search of food and raw materials. They found a range of different regions, from the grassy Great Plains to the drier areas of the southwest, all of which could be settled. At first they moved south, following the mammals, and hunting them with their stone-pointed spears. They also spread out east and west across the continent, finding more and better sources of flint for tools and weapons. Archaeologists have traced many of the stone tools to where they were first made. Some of them were carried hundreds, or even thousands, of kilometres, which shows how far the hunters journeyed.

It took several thousand years for the climate and vegetation to settle down into the pattern that still exists today. As this happened, species such as mammoths became extinct, and people turned to smaller animals for food. The hunters also developed lighter, more

accurate spears, which meant that they could bring down game without having to ambush it first. On the grasslands there were still large creatures, such as bison. These provided hunters with a number of different products, such as meat to eat, hides to make leather and bones for tools. From around 9000BC, the people of the plains, like those of other regions in North America, began to develop a lifestyle that would continue, with very little change, for many thousands of years.

The people of Asia, like the Europeans, took advantage of a better, more reliable food supply. They were healthier and their population began to increase. However, they still relied on many of their old techniques for survival and shelter. In some places, people started to settle down and build permanent huts. Elsewhere, hunters still built temporary shelters from branches or mammoth bones and hides.

As the ice thawed in Africa and the Middle East, many areas

◀ ANTLER HEADDRESS
Archaeologists found this unusual antler headdress at the British Stone Age site of Star Carr, Yorkshire. It may have been used in a religious ceremony or as a disguise when hunting deer.

HUNTERS' WEAPONS
By the late Ice Age, weapons had improved. Although spearheads and harpoon points were still made of stone, antler and bone, they were carefully carved so they worked well whenever they were used. When food was scarce, a hunter could not afford to lose his quarry because a blunt spear allowed an animal to escape.

▶ ANTLER POINTS
Hunters used deer antler to make deadly harpoon points. By carving away notches along one edge, then sharpening one or both ends, they made a barbed point. The advantage of this was that when a weapon was thrown at an animal it went in easily, but would not slip out as the creature ran away. Barbed points are still used by Arctic hunters.

◀ REPAIRING SPEARS
Stone spearheads such as North American Clovis points are virtually everlasting. But wooden spear shafts often break or split, so hunters had to fit their points to new ones. They fixed the points by splitting the shaft, jamming in the head, and binding animal sinew around the joint.

▼ HOME OF SKIN AND BONE
Like the people of the Ukraine, Siberian hunters built homes out of large animal bones and tusks, covered with skins and reinforced with timber if they could find it. Stones weighted down the skins on the ground. The people may have learned how to build these tents in the Ukraine before moving eastwards to their new homes.

that had been desert were covered with vegetation. Plants began to flourish in the Nile Valley and the eastern Mediterranean. This was a land of wild grasses, and people began to gather their seeds, grind them into flour and make bread to eat. One group of people who we know did this were the Natufians, a people who lived near the Wadi en-Natuf, in what is now Israel.

These cereal gatherers were learning a lot of vital information about the various kinds of corn. For example, which provided the tastiest grain, when best to harvest them and the most effective tools to use. Later, they would put this knowledge to good use, changing to a settled way of life and becoming some of the world's first farmers.

Removing flakes from the flint.

Carefully shaping the edge. The hand is protected by animal skin.

Putting the point into the cleft stick.

◄ MAKING A POINT
A hunter hit a lump of flint with an antler hammer, removing bits from either side until the piece was the right thickness and shape. Then he took a pointed piece of antler and worked around the edge of the point, removing chips to produce a razor-sharp edge. Next he put the point in a cleft stick and wrapped it around with sinews to protect it. He then hit the base of the point with his hammer, to remove a flake and make a fluted shape to fit the shaft.

Key Dates

- 10,000BC The Natufian culture develops in western Asia. Its people build round stone huts, herd goats, and gather wild emmer wheat.

- 9000BC Population levels begin to rise in Asia, encouraging people to take up new lifestyles such as herding.

- 9000BC People in America begin to hunt a wider range of smaller mammals. At the same time, a more settled lifestyle begins to evolve.

- 5000BC Tools in America become more specialized, and grindstones are created for processing plant foods.

- 3500BC People in North America begin to live in permanent villages.

Rock Paintings

▲ SAN HUNTERS
This modern rock painting by the San people, or bushmen, from the Kalahari Desert shows hunters chasing their quarry. It is one of many recent rock paintings done in a style similar to that used in prehistoric times.

UNLIKE CAVE PAINTINGS, which were hidden deep underground, rock paintings were made on rocks and cliff faces out in the open air. Some of these drawings are engraved into the rock with a sharp stone tool. Others are painted with natural pigments in a similar way to the cave paintings of the final Ice Age. Rock art occurs all over the world, from Africa to Australia. The drawings are usually easier to find than the cave paintings of western Europe, and in some places they are quite common. Some rock drawings date from 8000BC, but others were made as recently as the 1800s. The more recent pictures are often similar in style to the ancient images. This makes them difficult to date, but it also shows how the art and lifestyles of many peoples altered little until the early 1900s. Rock art can tell us a great deal about the lives of the people who created it – especially the creatures they hunted and farmed, because animals appear in these paintings more than any other subject.

Some of the most interesting and best preserved rock art is found in Africa. In the Saharan region, the types of animals in the pictures show how different the area was compared with the desert of today. After the final Ice Age, when the Sahara was covered in grasslands and dotted with oases

◀ HAND PAINTING
One method used by rock artists was to take some paint into the mouth and spit it on to the rock to produce a stencil of the hand.

THE VARIETY OF ROCK ART

The most common subjects in rock art are animals, people and patterns. Although the subjects are similar, the style of the pictures can vary greatly around the world. Some, like the paintings of the Sahara, are very realistic. Others, like the human figures of South America, are more like symbols than pictures of real people.

▶ GAZELLES
Artists from the Tassili Massif in the Sahara drew these gazelles. They were painted over 6,000 years ago. This was before the beginning of farming, when Saharan artists were still drawing the animals they hunted for food.

▲ BISON
The people of Bhimbetka, India, made rock drawings of animals for thousands of years. Bison, antelope and deer, as well as people, were popular subjects, and some, like this example, were filled in with delicate abstract patterns.

▲ HUMAN FIGURE
This rock engraving of a stylized person comes from Venezuela. No one knows what the circles and curves around it are, but they may be symbols of the Moon or Sun.

or shallow lakes, the area was home to wild oxen and gazelles. The local people hunted these animals and drew them on the walls of their shelters. After about 6000BC, they began to draw domestic cattle, showing that the change from hunting to farming near the oases happened around this time.

Other African paintings, such as those of the San people of what is now the Kalahari Desert, show hunters chasing their quarry. They are also shown fishing from their boats and gathering food. Pictures like these are almost certainly more than just decorations on shelter walls. The hunting pictures were probably produced as part of a ceremony performed before the hunt. The people hoped that drawing a successful hunt would make their own hunt turn out well. In a similar way, a picture of a group of men dancing around an antelope was probably intended to transfer some of the real animal's strength to the men of the tribe.

Paintings with a religious or ceremonial purpose are even more common in Australia. Stories of how the world was created have always been important to the native Australians. Each tribe has its own ancestor, usually an animal that is linked with some special part of the landscape. One Australian myth, which tells how the world was made, describes the way in which the rainbow serpent, who came from the sea, slithered on to the shore and created the landscape as he snaked his way inland. Rainbow serpents first begin to appear in rock paintings made by native Australians some 6,000 years ago.

▲ SPIRIT BEINGS
Australian rock painting represents spirits that were believed to be the ancestors of a particular tribe. They formed the focal point of the tribe's religious beliefs. The ancestors of different groups took different forms. Some were said to be animals, others were features of the landscape. They were all regarded with the deepest reverence by their people, as they are today.

◄ HUNTERS
Many rock drawings were made by hunting peoples, like these figures by the San people of the Kalahari Desert. The painted hunters seem to be moving with great agility, almost like dancers.

▶ LEAF
Depictions of plants are rarer in rock art than animals or people. They do occur occasionally, as in this Australian example from a site in the Northern Territory. Plant pictures may be linked to religion or the ancestors, or may have been done simply to create a decorative effect.

Key Dates

- 25,000BC Early inhabitants of Australia may be developing rock art.

- 20,000BC Rock artists may already be active in some parts of Africa.

- 11,000BC Rock art in central India shows hunters and prey.

- 8500BC The earliest rock paintings found in Saharan Africa portray wild animals.

- 8000BC The main period of cave painting ends in Europe. Rock art on cliffs and in shallower caves becomes common.

- 6000BC Saharan rock artists depict cattle, reflecting the change to the herding of livestock.

The First Farmers

▲ WHEAT
Finding a staple crop that provides basic energy needs is an important step in farming. Wheat is one of the most common. Others are millet, rice and maize.

HUNTERS AND GATHERERS were highly skilled at finding food. However, their success was dependent on the weather, local conditions and luck. If the weather turned bad, or the local supplies ran out, people faced starvation. Around 11,000 years ago, a group of people in the Middle East changed this. They began to produce their own food by farming. It was one of the most important developments in the history of humankind.

Farming gave people control over their food supply. They did not have to wander through the countryside looking for food any longer. They could settle in one place, and as a result began to build stronger, more comfortable houses than before. Farming also offered a more reliable supply of food, although in years when the harvest was bad, people had to return to gathering for a while.

The first farmers lived at the eastern end of the Mediterranean (now Israel, Palestine and Syria) and in an upland region north of the River Tigris in what now forms parts of Iran and Iraq. This region has more rain than the surrounding plains and grasses such as wheat and barley grow there naturally. Because of its climate and its shape on the map, the area is now known as the Fertile Crescent.

The people of the Fertile Crescent had gathered wheat seeds for thousands of years. They knew which types grew most vigorously and produced the best grain. By about 9000BC, they realized that they could plant these grasses and harvest them. At around the same time, they started to herd the wild sheep and goats. These animals provided milk and wool as well as meat. During the next 3,000 years, people also began to keep livestock, pigs and cattle.

In good years, farming gave the people of the Fertile Crescent more food than they

◀ STONE TOWER
Jericho's tallest building was a stone tower. No one knows why the tower was built. It could have been a watchtower, or it might have had some religious purpose.

THE FARMERS' WORLD

Although farming created a lot of hard work, the people of the first agricultural villages did not spend all their time in the fields. In many places, they developed quite complex religious beliefs and ceremonies. They produced new styles of art, including sculptures made from plaster and pottery decorated with striking abstract designs of lines and rectangles. They also started to make larger baskets and clay containers for storing surplus corn.

◀ FIGURE SCULPTURE
The world's earliest large-scale human sculptures were produced in Ain Ghazal, Jordan. They were shaped in lime plaster over a skeleton of straw bundles. The eyes were outlined with dark paint. No one knows why they were made.

▶ SPOUTED BOWL
From the early farming site at Khirokitia, Cyprus, came this decorated pottery bowl. It was buried in the grave of an eight-year-old child, and was obviously a well-loved object, as it had been repaired before the burial.

◀ PLASTERED SKULL
Around 6000BC, the religious ceremonies of Jericho involved the use of human skulls. The skulls were covered with plaster, which was shaped to copy the person's ears, nose, mouth and other facial features. Cowrie shells were placed in the eye sockets, and teeth were added.

could eat. They stored the surplus in grain bins or baskets, and traded it for materials, for tools, or items such as pots and furniture.

Gradually, the farmers and craftworkers became rich. They built more and bigger houses clustered together. These groups of houses developed into small towns. The houses were made of mud-bricks, providing warmth in winter while staying cool in summer. One of the first of these towns was Jericho, built near a spring north of the Dead Sea. The land around the town was good both for growing crops and for grazing herds and flocks of animals, and soon Jericho became prosperous. It was not long before other towns were built in this area.

As farming spread further afield, it was not very long before other regions began to produce their food in a similar way, and the pattern of human life had changed for ever.

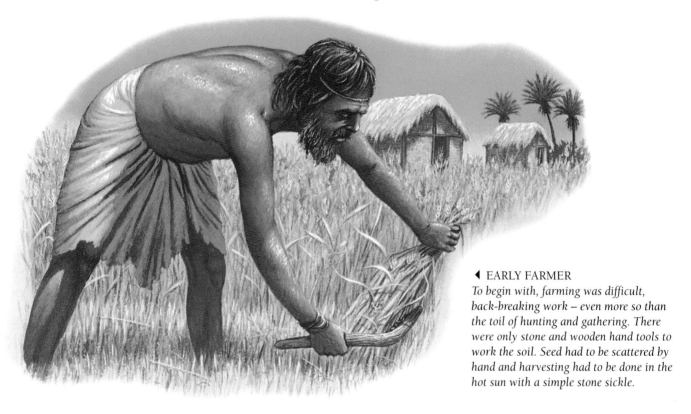

◀ EARLY FARMER
To begin with, farming was difficult, back-breaking work – even more so than the toil of hunting and gathering. There were only stone and wooden hand tools to work the soil. Seed had to be scattered by hand and harvesting had to be done in the hot sun with a simple stone sickle.

◀ FARMING IN THE FERTILE CRESCENT
To begin with, farming was most successful where there were light soils. These could be easily worked with basic hand tools. There also had to be plants growing wild that were suitable for cultivating. From its beginnings near the Persian Gulf, the River Euphrates and the eastern Mediterranean, farming spread gradually outwards. Egypt to the south and Turkey and Greece to the north-west were places where farming arrived early.

Key Dates

- 10,000BC Cereal gathering begins in Palestine.

- 9000BC Farming begins in the Fertile Crescent.

- 9000BC The people of Syria and nearby regions sow wheat.

- 9000BC Jericho develops as a small settlement around a spring.

- 8000BC Animal herding is well established in the Zagros Mountains.

- 7000BC Cereal farming is widespread from Turkey to the Fertile Crescent, in the Zagros Mountains and parts of Pakistan.

Plants and Animals

Early farmers in the Fertile Crescent used the date palm for its fruit, wood, leaves and fibres.

THE FIRST FARMERS DID NOT simply take wild grasses and plant them in rows in their fields. They had to work hard to turn the wild species they found into true cereal crops. To begin with, they had to choose the plants that were the most suitable for food. In Europe and Asia, farmers chose grasses such as wheat and barley. Farmers in eastern Asia grew millet. Tropical African growers cultivated yams. The first farmers in North America selected corn, while those in South America chose potatoes and another root vegetable, manioc.

Farmers watched out for the individual plants that were strongest or biggest. American corn farmers, for example, collected the seed from plants yielding the biggest cobs, and sowed these, to produce a crop with larger cobs next year.

Farmers in the Fertile Crescent had a different problem with their wheat. One species that grew well was wild einkorn wheat. But its seeds tended to break off and fall to the ground when they ripened, making them difficult to harvest. Eventually the farmers noticed that a few plants had seeds that did not fall so quickly, so they bred their crops from these. Soon they had

▼ CATTLE ROCK PAINTING
When the people of the Sahara began to farm, their artists started to paint pictures of cattle. This example shows a herd of cattle, of the type that were kept more than 4,000 years ago. The painting also includes some of the people who herded them. It comes from a site in the Tassili mountains, in the central Sahara.

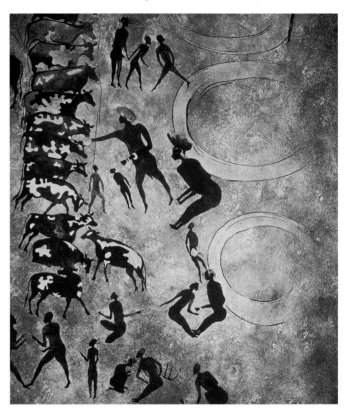

ON EARLY FARMS

Early farms looked quite unlike modern ones. The animals and plants were different, the farmer and his family usually shared their house with the animals. There were no machines, just simple tools and a lot of hard work. The whole family helped, especially at busy times such as harvest. Even young children lent a hand, which was good training for when they would be farmers themselves.

wild einkorn

domestic einkorn

auroch

cattle

◀ WILD AND DOMESTIC WHEAT
The main difference between wild and domestic einkorn wheat is the seeds. In the domestic variety these are much larger. The plant's stalk is also stronger, which stops the seeds from falling off before the harvest.

▶ WILD AND DOMESTIC CORN
Modern domestic corn has a larger seed cob than the ancient wild variety. Early farmers probably bred corn cobs that were larger than the wild varieties but not as big as today's giant cobs.

wild corn

domestic corn

◀ WILD AND DOMESTIC CATTLE
The wild auroch was the ancestor of early farm cattle. Bones found by archaeologists show early domesticated cattle were smaller than the wild ones. But early farmers probably tried different sizes of cattle to see which suited them best.

◀ A FARMING VILLAGE
The first farming villages in Turkey were small clusters of mud-brick houses, where people and animals lived close together for safety. In the hot dry summers, the village streets were baked hard and dusty, but in the winter they became a mass of puddles and sticky mud. These farmers kept goats, and cattle descended from the wild aurochs.

developed a new species, domesticated einkorn wheat, with seeds that only broke away during threshing.

Early farmers bred their animals in a similar way, selecting the beasts with the features they wanted, and breeding from them. But the changes to the animal species were less dramatic than with the crops. The pigs farmed in the Fertile Crescent, for example, were much smaller and more like wild boars than modern domestic pigs. Cattle too were smaller than modern cows, and sheep and goats looked like the wild species.

Most early domestic animals were smaller than their wild cousins. This is probably because farmers bred good-tempered, docile creatures that were less aggressive and easier to handle than wild animals. Rather than choosing large specimens, farmers would have selected animals that produced the best-tasting meat or the highest yield of milk. Gradually, the farmers built up knowledge and experience, and must have discovered that the smaller animals often had the features they wanted.

▲ PLANT DOMESTICATION
Farmers in different parts of the world grew different types of crops. In each area, one or two crops became the most commonly grown. They were varieties that were easy to grow in that particular area and provided a good basic crop.

Key Dates

- 9000BC Sheep domesticated in northern Mesopotamia.

- 8000BC First domesticated cereals grown around Jericho.

- 7000 BC Sheep and goats kept in the eastern Mediterranean.

- 7000BC Barley grown in the Fertile Crescent. Emmer wheat in Palestine. Einkorn wheat in Turkey and Mesopotamia.

- 7000BC Pigs are domesticated in southern Turkey.

- 6000BC Cattle kept by farmers in north Africa and the eastern Mediterranean.

The Coming of Trade

▲ DAGGER
This dagger, with its long flint blade and its snake-shaped handle, was probably made for decorative effect rather than use in battle.

FARMING MADE SOME PEOPLE well-fed, rich and successful. They could trade the extra food they produced in exchange for luxury goods. Soon, this became a way of life for many farmers and trading towns began to appear in the Fertile Cresecent and in Anatolia (Turkey). Most of these early towns disappeared long ago. As one set of mud-brick buildings fell into disrepair, they were knocked down. People built new houses on top of the old foundations. This happened many times over hundreds of years, and the town's ground level gradually rose as each group of houses was replaced. When a town was finally abandoned, the ruins, with their build-up of floor levels, was left in the form of a mound. In Syria and Palestine this type of ancient mound is called a tell. In Turkey it is known as a hüyük.

One of the most famous of these early town mounds is Çatal Hüyük in central Turkey. When archaeologists began to dig this mound, they found that it concealed an ancient town, occupied by a trading people who lived there between 7000 and

▶ BUILDING WORK
Clay was the main material for building in early trading towns of the Middle East. It could be pressed into brick shapes while wet and left to dry in the sun. Surfaces were plastered to give a weatherproof finish outside and a smooth surface for decoration within.

6000BC. The countryside around the town was rich farming land. Charred remains from the town have shown that the people grew wheat, barley, lentils and other vegetables, as well as eating such fruit as apples and wild nuts such as almonds.

The people of Çatal Hüyük probably traded in food products and raw materials for making tools. A preferred material was obsidian, a black glass, formed naturally in volcanoes. Archaeologists have found a range of different tools and weapons made of flint and obsidian on the site.

The houses of Çatal Hüyük were built of mud-brick. They were square or rectangular, and built close together. One amazing feature of the town was that it had no streets. People entered their houses from the flat

MYSTERIES OF A TURKISH TOWN

There are still many mysteries surrounding the town of Çatal Hüyük in central Turkey in spite of all the work of the archaeologists. No one knows for sure the meaning of the wall paintings in many of the rooms that have been excavated. The bulls, birds, leopards and human figures were probably gods. However, it is not clear what the gods stood for, or how they were worshipped.

▲ BULL PAINTING
This mural is from a shrine at Çatal Hüyük. It shows a group of people baiting a gigantic bull. Bulls had religious significance because they were associated with a male god.

▶ CLAY SEALS
Oval-shaped stamps with abstract patterns may have been used as seals. Each person would have had a seal with a different design and used it to mark his or her property, as proof of ownership.

▶ BIRD WALL-PAINTING
These birds are probably vultures. People in some cultures left their dead out of doors, until vultures had picked away the flesh.

roofs, stepping down wooden ladders to the floor below. Defending such places was easy.

Many houses contained at least one room set aside for religious ceremonies. These rooms, or shrines, are decorated with bulls' heads made of plaster and fitted with real bulls' horns. They also have wall paintings of animals and figures. Many of the figures are female, and archaeologists have also found more than 50 small

statues of pregnant women, suggesting that the people worshipped a mother goddess.

In addition, the shrines contain platforms that may have been used as altars in some form of religious ceremony. When residents of Çatal Hüyük died, their bodies were left in the open air, where the flesh was removed by the vultures. Then their relatives brought the bones back into the town and buried them beneath these platforms.

Ladder gives access to roof

Flat roof provides work space and route to adjoining houses

Decorated room used as religious shrine

Roof made of layers of timber, reeds and mud

◀ TOWN HOUSES
Houses at Çatal Hüyük were made mainly from mud-brick. This material was even used for fittings like benches and hearths. The houses were packed closely together with only a few courtyards between them. This made the town compact and helped to make it easier to defend, with few corners where enemies or wild beasts could lurk.

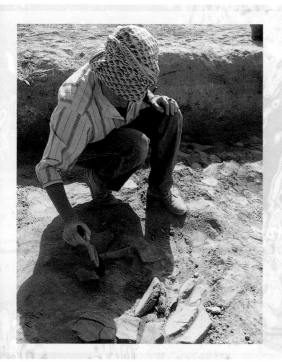

◀ EXCAVATING A SITE
The most common way for archaeologists to dig is to make a trench, a rectangular hole across the site. They can find remains from different periods because they lie in bands like a layer cake, revealing small areas across a broad time span. When there are many remains of buildings and other structures, such as at Çatal Hüyük, archaeologists will sometimes excavate to a shallow depth, over a broader area to cover more of the site.

Key Dates

- 8000BC Trade begins to develops in the Fertile Crescent and Anatolia.
- 7000BC Çatal Hüyük becomes important as a town and trading hub.
- 7000BC Jericho expands; religious rituals include decorating skulls with plaster and shells.
- 6800BC Pottery is widely used in the eastern Mediterranean.
- 6500BC More elaborate burials at settlements such as Çatal Hüyük and Jericho show that some people were more important than others.
- 5000BC Trade links established between Turkey and the eastern Mediterranean.

Pots and Potters

▲ PAINTED POTTERY
The earliest pottery was plain, but potters soon learned how to paint their wares to make them more attractive. This pot is from an early farming community in Europe.

WE TAKE POTTERY, SUCH as cups, bowls, mugs and plates for granted. Before pottery was invented, our earliest ancestors used hollowed out stone containers and woven baskets. The first pottery was probably made around 10,500BC. Pots are made from clay, which was dug from the ground, so they are cheap. They could be made in a variety of shapes and sizes, and hold liquids as well as dry foods. Once people had discovered how to make pots, they never stopped finding new uses for them.

Pottery was probably discovered by accident. Early peoples baked bread and other foods in ovens which they made from earth. They piled up a mound of clay and made a hollow in which they lit a fire. Inside, it became very hot. Eventually someone must have noticed that the sides of the clay oven had hardened with the heat.

It was probably some time before anyone had the idea of using this hardened clay to make containers. The earliest pots so far discovered come from Japan. From Japan, knowledge of pottery may have spread to China, where slightly more recent vessels have been found. However, in the rest of Asia, Europe and Africa, pottery is much more recent. It is possible that it may have been discovered independently, as it was in America.

The first pots were made by the coiling process. The potter made a long, thin sausage of clay and looped it in a circle, working upwards to make the sides of the pot. Another ancient technique was to form pots by using a stone template that was removed when the potter achieved the right shape. Much later, some time after 3000BC, the potter's wheel was invented. This device is still used by potters all over

◀ TERRACOTTA FIGURE
Pottery can be formed into all sorts of shapes, not only containers. People soon realized that they could use it to make small, portable statues. These were common among early farming communities, and archaeologists have excavated shrines with large numbers of these figures.

POTS AND POTTERS

In hunter-gatherer societies, people generally collected food as they needed it. Farming produced a glut of food at harvest time. People now needed containers to store this food, so pottery and farming flourished at the same time. The earliest pottery is unglazed. This means that it absorbs moisture, so that it is best used for dry goods such as grain and other solid foods.

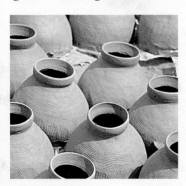

◀ UNGLAZED POTS
Simple unglazed storage jars are still made in many parts of the world. These jars, elegantly shaped and decorated with patterns made by the potters' fingertips, come from Ghana. Pots like this are sometimes given a decorative glaze.

▲ ROUND-BASED POT
This is one of the oldest pots so far discovered by archaeologists. It comes from Nasunahara, Japan, and dates to around 10,500BC. The pot has a beaded pattern in bands around the rim.

▶ JOMON POT, JAPAN
Jomon or cord-marked pottery was produced in Japan around 10,000BC. The clay was coiled into shape and the pots had pointed bases. They were probably hardened by heating on an open fire, rather than by firing in an enclosed kiln like later pots. This pot, used as a storage jar, stands about 23cm/9in high.

the world. The finished pots were fired and hardened in a kiln, which was similar to an ancient oven.

One advantage of pottery is that it is extremely long-lasting, and has survived to provide evidence for archaeologists. Each region and period has its own style of pottery. The shade of the clay, the thickness of the pot, the style of decoration all vary from place to place and time to time. An archaeologist can often tell, even from a fragment of pottery, when and where it was made. They can therefore give a date to the sites where they find pots. Pots of foreign origin also provide clues as to trade and links between various countries.

▲ POTTERS AT WORK

The potter in the foreground is making a pot by coiling clay. With help from her daughter, she has prepared long, sausage-shaped pieces of clay and wound them around to build up the shape of the vessel. When she is happy with the overall shape, she will moisten her fingers and rub the surface of the pot to make it smooth. She may then make handles and stick them to the sides.

▲ EARLY POTTERY SITES

Archaeologists have discovered many remains of both early pottery and kilns in China and Japan. These areas continued to be at the forefront of developments in pottery until the 1800s. Kilns, glazing and, much later, waterproof porcelain, were all discovered and first used in the Far East.

Key Dates

- 10,500BC First Japanese pottery.

- 7000BC Unbaked, sun-dried clay vessels made in Syria and Turkey.

- 7000BC Hunter-fishers of southern Sahara are the first potters in Africa.

- 6500BC First European pottery.

- 6000BC Fishing communities in southern China make pottery.

- 3500BC The tournette, a simple device for turning a pot, appears in Mesopotamia and Egypt.

- 3000BC Potter's wheel invented in the Middle East.

- 1500BC Glazed pottery that is resistant to water made in China.

European Settlements

▲ GREEK HOUSE
Early Greek farmers built small one-roomed houses with sloping thatched roofs. They often included a clay bin so that they could store their grain indoors. This house is from the village of Nea Nikomedeia in Greece.

FARMING SEEMS TO HAVE spread to Europe from the east, from around 7000BC. It reached Europe from Turkey and then spread westwards towards the Atlantic coast.

Then, as now, the European climate and landscape varied greatly. In the Balkans, where farming in Europe started, it was dry, and the land was suitable for sheep and goats, as well as for cereal growing. In northern Europe, early farmers led a very different life. The weather was colder, the soil heavier and much of the ground was covered with forest. This was not good country for sheep and goats, so pig-rearing and cattle-herding were more popular. People could grow cereal crops, but the heavier soil was harder to cultivate than in the south. Gradually, over many centuries, the northerners developed strains of cereals that could grow in the heavy soil.

The woods of the north had many benefits. They were good foraging-grounds for pigs, and also provided a variety of food plants for people. They also sheltered animals such as deer and wild boar that could be hunted for both food and skins. The northern

Europeans continued to hunt and gather to add variety to the food they produced on their farms.

The plentiful timber was also useful for building. The farmers of central and northern Europe cut down trees to make a stout framework for the walls and roofs

▲ FARMING SETTLEMENT
A small farming village in western Britain consisted of a few round thatched houses clustered together. Next to the houses were fields for animals and crops. A trackway gave access to the fields and connected this village with others.

CRAFTS OF THE FARMERS
With the settled way of life that came with farming, people began to develop their craft skills. Among the most important were building and pottery. These early farmers were skilled woodworkers. They made fences, tools and containers.

face pot, Hungary

Bandkeramik pot, Germany

▲ RAISED PATHWAY
People sometimes built farming villages in marshy land. They made wooden walkways raised on posts so that they could cross the swamps safely.

▲ DECORATED POTS
Potters decorated pots by drawing patterns or simplified faces in the damp clay. Another design was made up of lines and dots in a style known by the German name *Bandkeramik*, meaning "banded pottery".

▲ SEATED FIGURE
This pottery statuette from a farming site in Hungary shows a man holding a sickle. He may be a corn god, or just an ordinary farmer.

of their homes. They used split logs to make the walls and plastered them over with daub, a mixture of mud and straw, to fill the gaps. This helped to keep out draughts. The roofs, which had a steep pitch to throw off snow and rain, were thatched. Some of these houses were up to 45m/150ft in length and are known as longhouses. They were Europe's first sizeable, permanent dwellings. As well as a large room for the family, they usually also contained a store-room

for crops and an area for cattle. Sometimes humans and animals shared the same room. It was cramped and smelly, but people put up with this to make sure their animals were safe.

Farming villages became established in many river valleys. People used the rivers to travel between nearby villages to trade. Along the way, they also exchanged ideas about new discoveries and inventions. As a result, pottery techniques and styles improved and spread, and new ideas about crop and animal cultivation were shared. The people of Europe were developing skills which would stay in use for thousands of years.

◀ EUROPEAN FARMERS

At Langweiler, Germany, farmers build a longhouse for their family and animals. They have constructed the walls and are now thatching the roof. To do this they have gathered reeds from a nearby river. Reeds make a longer-lasting thatch than grass or straw.

▲ FARMING REACHES EUROPE

From the Middle East and Turkey, farming spread gradually west along coasts and river valleys. The three main areas of farming in Europe were the Balkans, the Mediterranean coast, and north and west Europe, to which farming came last.

Key Dates

- 7000BC Farming reaches eastern Europe, probably from Turkey.

- 6200BC Farming begins in Sicily and southern Italy.

- 5400BC Farming spreads across northern Europe, from Hungary, through Germany to the Netherlands.

- 5000BC Farming communities such as Langweiler are thriving.

- 5000BC Farming has spread across southern Europe and has reached the south of France.

- 4000BC Farming established in most of Europe.

Asian Communities

▲ HARPOON
HEADS, CHINA
*Items like these bone
harpoon points from
the farming site at
Banpo, China, show
that hunting and river
fishing were still key
sources of food.*

GOOD SOIL AND USEFUL LOCAL
crops encouraged Asian
people to begin farming.
This is how agriculture began in
eastern Asia, in places like the
highlands of north-west and
central India, and areas around the
banks of the Yellow River in China.
Both regions had good natural
resources and a climate suitable for
farming. Archaeologists have found
the remains of several early farming
villages in both places.

Central India had grassy
uplands suitable for cattle grazing
and river banks with rich soil for
crops. Farming began early here,
around 7000BC. Barley was a
popular crop, and farmers herded
cattle, goats and sheep on the hills.

In some places, people gathered
together to build villages. One of the first was called
Mehrgarh, a cluster of houses by the River Bolan in
north-west India. The houses were square or
rectangular, and built of mud-bricks plastered with
mud. The flat roofs were made of reed thatch supported
on long wooden poles. Inside, there were several
rooms. Thick walls and small windows kept

▲ RICE FARMER
*When the people had worked out how to cultivate the waterlogged
fields of southern China and south-east Asia, rice became the
staple crop of these areas.*

the houses warm in winter and cool in summer. The
style remained much the same for the next 1,000 years.

Communities like Mehrgarh grew. People built
storehouses for grain to ensure a reserve when supplies
became short. Some members of the community grew
rich, perhaps by trading. Their graves contain cherished
possessions, such as beads of shell or limestone.

Meanwhile, agriculture was developing in China.
Here, millet was the preferred crop, and the pig was the

SUCCESSFUL FARMERS
Successful farmers could grow more food than
they needed, and could therefore trade with
others. They began to own luxury items such as
ornamentation and finer, decorated pots. When
archaeologists excavate items like these, they
know that they must have belonged to a very
wealthy person.

◄ WATER JAR
An amphora jar, from Banpo, China, has a
narrow neck, which means it was
designed to hold liquid. A rope was
threaded between the two loop handles
so that it could be carried easily, and
rested on a stand or embedded
upright in the soil.

◄ POTTERY LID
This decorative lid, with
a knob in the shape of a
human face, was found at
Banshan, a farming village
in north-west China. It is
around 20cm/8in across and is
an example of the kind of
items owned by people
who were rich or had
high social rank.

▶ YANGSHAO
POTTERY
Later Chinese
farmers, around
3000BC, produced
several different
styles of pottery.
One type, called
Yangshao, is finely
painted, like these two
decorated bowls.

first creature to be domesticated. Farmers also grew vegetables such as cabbages, and harvested fruit such as plums. Later, they began to grow rice, which became the staple in most of eastern Asia. Rice was especially successful in southern China, where the ground was wetter.

Chinese farmers quickly learned that their soils needed a rest after a season of cultivation. They developed a method of farming that switched from one field to another. This allowed the land to have a fallow period, where the land was not worked or sown. They found that by leaving a long fallow period between periods of growing, the land could be restored. Much later, around 1100BC, they began to alternate crops of millet and soya beans. The bean plants brought goodness back to the soil, meaning that it was less important to have a fallow period.

Techniques of farming spread steadily across China. Wet farming techniques needed for rice were passed from south to north, along with strains of rice that grew more successfully in the north. China also had contact with Korea and Japan. These two areas had successful hunting and fishing communities. Agriculture did not become established there until much later.

Straw thatch

Plastered wall

Supporting pole

Central hearth

▲ FARMER'S HUT, BANPO
Chinese archaeologists found the remains of a cluster of houses belonging to the early farming community of Banpo in northern China, dating from about 6000BC. The buildings were oblong or round. They were built with a stout wooden framework filled in with a basket-weave of thin branches. This was plastered over to make a smooth, weather-resistant wall. Thatch covered the roofs, but there was a central hole to let smoke escape from the fire in the floor below.

Wooden poles support reed thatch

▲ MUD-BRICK HOUSE
One of India's oldest farming villages is Mehrgarh, by the River Bolan in north-west India. The houses are mostly square, have several rooms and are made of plastered mud-bricks.

▼ BURIAL
The dead at Mehrgarh in north-west India were buried in free areas in the village itself. The bodies were positioned on their sides, their knees bent. Grave goods were placed with them. Rich people's graves contained items such as stone and shell beads.

Key Dates

- 7000BC Barley growing begins in India.

- 6000BC Indian farmers start building storehouses for their surplus food.

- 6000BC Millet is the main crop of farmers in northern China.

- 5500BC Date palms are cultivated in Mesopotamia.

- 5500BC Indian farmers produce their own strains of wheat.

- 5000BC Farmers of the Yangtze Delta area cultivate rice.

- 3500BC Trade networks link the regions of China.

- 3000BC Millet grown in Korea.

The Americas

▲ DEER FIGURE
People of south-western North America made figures like this split-twig deer. These figures date to a period after 3500BC and are often found near hunters' weapons and equipment.

WHETHER THEY WERE fishing or harpooning seals in the far north, hunting bison on the Great Plains, or gathering food in the south, the people of the Americas followed the food supply. As crops grew in the least extreme weather conditions, they also had to move with the seasons. They became used to a restless life.

In Central America, environmental changes were often fast and unpredictable. Torrential rain was followed by baking sun. The people here longed for more control over their food supply, and turned to agriculture before the rest of the Americas. However, they still needed good weather for their crops, which is perhaps why so many of them worshipped gods of rain and sun. The farmers hoped that worshipping these deities would bring them the best conditions throughout the agricultural year.

One of the earliest crops in Central America was corn (maize), a plant which has been important in American farming ever since. It was developed from a local wild grass called teosinte. Farmers tried different

▲ HUT AND HUNTER
In eastern North America, hunters often built short-term shelters, like this hut. They made a framework of thin wooden poles, joined together at the top. This they covered with grass. Huts like this could catch fire easily, so the hearth was outside.

varieties, choosing the plants that grew best in local conditions. This proved successful approach, and maize farming spread quite quickly.

Further north, in what is now the south-west USA, the first farmers experimented with various types of gourd and with plants such as sunflower and sumpweed. As the farmers of Central America began to trade more widely, they took their domesticated maize, beans and squash with them, and these joined the local

AMERICAN FARMERS

The Americas contain a variety of different climates and environments, all with their own native plant species. For the early farmers, the challenge was to choose the best plants for their own region. Often this was simply a question of selecting from local species that were known to do well. But sometimes an imported crop, such as cotton in southern North America, was a success.

◄ POTATOES
Between 3000 and 2500BC, farmers in the hills of the Andes were growing the potato. For thousands of years, this useful root crop was grown only in South America, and many varieties of potato are still found only in the Andes.

▲ STONE WEIGHTS
Hunters in Kentucky attached these stone weights to the handles of their spear-throwers. This made their spears travel much farther and faster. As a result, when a spear hit an animal it was much more powerful.

◄ CLAY FIGURINE
Mysterious statuettes like this one have been found in numerous North American settlements. They have little in the way of shaping or facial features, so it is impossible to tell whether they represent male or female figures. They are made of clay and decorated with lines and dots. The clay was not fired, though, it simply became hard with age. No one knows what these figures were for.

plants to become staple crops in the north. For many people in the south-west, the plants were a welcome addition to foraged foods.

In South America people tried to cultivate a variety of crops, including gourds, squashes, manioc, potatoes and various types of bean. In each area, they selected the best plants for local conditions and tried different growing methods over thousands of years. The region where farming caught on most quickly was Peru. In the Andes mountains, hunter-gatherers began to grow crops such as gourds and beans to add to their existing

diet. They carried on using this mixed form of food supply for many thousands of years.

In the coastal areas, rivers had created narrow valleys as they flowed off the mountains to the sea. In the rich soil found in these valleys, people began to grow squashes and peppers, to which they later added maize. They also developed methods of irrigation to bring water from the rivers to their fields.

Animal farming was at first less popular in the Americas than in other parts of the world. There were few native species that were easy to farm. But in the Andes mountains one species, the llama, was valued for its wool and milk, as well as being used as a beast of burden. The people of the Americas developed a variety of crops and farming techniques, but in many places wild foods were still widely available and many groups carried on their lifestyle of hunting and gathering.

▼ RIVER TRANSPORT
Simple wooden canoes provided transport along North America's rivers. There were various ways of making these. They could be "dug-outs", made by hollowing out a log. Another design was made of thin tree bark attached to a wooden frame.

▼ SUNFLOWERS
This giant member of the daisy family is found mainly in North America. Farmers prized it for its seeds, which can be eaten. Later they learned how to extract the oil from the seeds, using it for cooking. Some species also have edible roots.

▶ COTTON
This valuable crop was first cultivated in two separate areas, Peru and Ecuador in South America and Mexico in Central America. From Mexico, traders brought it to the North American south-west, where farmers later began to grow the plant.

Key Dates

- 8500BC Agriculture established in Peru. Crops grown include squash, beans and grasses.

- 7000BC In Central America people gather avocado, chilli, squash and beans. These are plants farmers will begin to cultivate in the next 2,000 years.

- 6300BC Farmers in Peru grow various root crops, such as oca and ulluco.

- 5400BC The use of llamas for wool, milk and transport is common in the Andes.

- 5000BC Mexican farmers grow maize.

- 5000BC Domesticated plants of Central America, such as the bottle gourd, begin to spread to North America.

Hunting and Gathering

▲ GIRAFFE
Artists painted both farm animals and the hunters' preferred quarry on the walls of rock shelters in the Sahara Desert. The giraffe was one of the creatures that people living in Africa both herded and hunted during prehistoric times.

FARMING WAS NOT FOR everyone. Hunting and gathering can provide a steady, reliable source of food as long as there are not too many people living in a small area. Africa is one part of the world where some peoples made the change to farming, while others continued to hunt and gather for much longer.

After the final Ice Age, the Sahara was a much damper, greener environment than it is today. It became the scene for some of Africa's earliest experiments in farming. Rock paintings show how the people began to herd cattle, together with other local species such as giraffe.

When the Sahara dried out and gradually turned to desert, most agricultural activity was pushed to the south, between the Sahara and the Equator. This was where the climate allowed farmers to develop crops such as yam and sorghum, a cereal crop that was suited to warm places. This area became the heartland of African farming.

Still further south, people carried on hunting and gathering. They ate a number of local plants, especially various palms and a shrub called bauhinia. In addition, they found out how to use other plants for more specialized purposes. A good example was the bottle gourd, which was suitable for making into containers.

The African hunter-gatherers also improved their tools. To make knives, they used tiny blades of sharp flint, which they glued into wooden handles using natural tree resin. They also carved hooks from bone for fishing. Such uses of the materials around them show how highly adapted they were to their environment.

Australia was another place where the traditional lifestyle of hunting and gathering continued. To begin with,

◀ TRADITIONAL HUNTER
Today, some African peoples still get some of their food by hunting, but now their spears are tipped with metal rather than the stone of earlier times.

USEFUL SPECIES

The early hunter-gatherers of Africa and Australia had a vast knowledge of plants. When they came across a new species they would try it out. This was a dangerous process, as many plants were poisonous. They gradually discovered plants that were good to eat and others that worked as medicines. Modern scientists are still investigating the plant medicines used by the world's hunter-gatherer peoples.

◀ ALMONDS
Nuts, such as almonds, that are native to North Africa and the Middle East, are a nutritious food. Gatherers made a point of going to the forest when they were in season. They are easy to store and contain plenty of energy-building protein, useful to hunter-gatherers when meat was in short supply.

▶ JUNIPER BERRIES
Gatherers soon knew everything about the plants in their area. They discovered that some plants, though not good to eat, had other useful properties. Berries like juniper, which grows all over the northern hemisphere, were valued for their perfume and their use in medicine.

◀ GOURD
Some species of gourd were very useful. When the flesh had been eaten, the outer shells made excellent containers. People made bowls with the larger fruit, while using smaller ones to make items such as dippers and cups.

people stayed near the coast, living on fish, eels and, especially, shellfish. Remains of the shells, left in dumps that archaeologists call middens, have been found along both the north and south-east coasts. As time went on, the native Australians explored the river valleys, moving gradually inland. People discovered that cereal plants such as millet made good food. They developed hunting skills that enabled them to survive when they moved even further inland towards Australia's hot and dry interior.

The early Australians roamed for miles, exchanging tools and shell ornaments, and creating the beautiful rock art, which can still be found all over the country. As they did this, they were also developing a complex series of myths about their ancestry that reflected their hunting and gathering lifestyle. Most important of all are the stories of Dreamtime, the period when the earth and the spirits of people were created. These myths held, and still hold, great religious significance for native Australians, and reveal a people of profound beliefs.

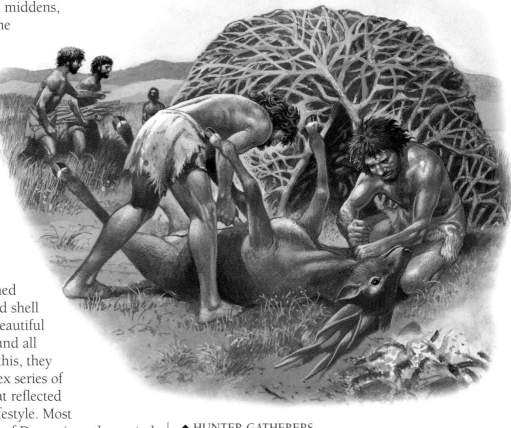

▲ HUNTER-GATHERERS
This group of hunter-gatherers have found an area rich in food and have made a camp with a brushwood shelter that they will occupy for weeks or even months. While two men butcher the antelope they have killed, another group of people returns from gathering vegetables and wood for the fire on which they will cook the meat.

▼ ENGRAVED PEARL SHELL
In societies that did not use metals, all sorts of items were adapted for use as ornamentation. This example, engraved with abstract designs, was made by native Australians from a piece of pearl shell.

◀ BARK PAINTING
A hunter throws his spear at a crane in this bark painting from Australia's Northern Territory. This style of painting is known as "x-ray", because the designs on the crane depict the bird's insides.

Key Dates

- 10,000BC Obsidian, a type of volcanic glass, used to make tools in the Rift Valley area of eastern Africa.

- 9000BC People move into the Sahara region; increased rainfall allows grasslands to grow along the edges of what is now desert.

- 7000BC African communities in the Sahara begin making pottery.

- 6000BC People start herding cattle in some parts of the Sahara region.

- 4000BC Sahara reaches its wettest, most temperate conditions, with Lake Chad at its largest.

- 3500BC Ostrich egg-shell beads become popular as necklaces in eastern Africa.

The First Metalworkers

▲ GOLD BULL
The settlement of Varna, on the Black Sea, was one of Europe's first metal-working sites. Hundreds of gold ornaments, bracelets and beads have been discovered there.

As they created art on to surfaces in caves, ancient peoples must have seen gold. They would also have seen copper, as it has a greenish tinge in the rock. Deposits of metal in rock are rare, and difficult to extract. It was a long time before anyone worked out how to remove the material and then to work it into something useful. Eventually, someone found a place where there was enough metal to remove and found that it could be hammered into shape. Metal was beaten into ornamental objects such as beads, which were soon highly valued.

When craftworkers started to make pottery, they built kilns that could reach temperatures as high as 800°C/1500°F. Before long, they found that heating certain rocks, or ores, in the kiln melted the metal they contained, so that it could be poured off and collected. They had discovered the process called smelting. This made it possible to extract much larger amounts of metal from the ore. People could make all sorts of items out of copper rather than other materials. There was

▲ BRONZE AGE SETTLEMENT
Most of the people of Bronze Age Europe lived in small villages with thatched houses, like those built by the first farmers. An area would be set aside for metalworking away from the houses, so that there was less risk of fire.

THE MAGIC OF METAL
The first metals must have seemed like magic. By heating the ore, the metalworker could make metal appear, apparently out of nowhere. It would first be seen in hot liquid form, then it would miraculously set when it cooled. Copper and gold glittered beautifully in the light, so people found these metals very attractive.

▼ LONG-HORNED OXEN
Small, precious objects were among the first items to be made of metal, because they did not use very much of it. Early metalworkers could produce objects of great skill, as these copper oxen found in Poland demonstrate.

mould

pin

◀ MOULD AND PIN
A Bronze Age mould and matching pin show how the process of casting could be used to produce a number of items at speed – in this case three pins at the same time. The small holes at each corner would have matched with bumps in the other half of the mould, to ensure a perfect fit.

▶ COPPER AND TIN
The first important alloy was bronze, a mix of copper and tin. Tin is not common, so bronze developed slowly where there were good tin deposits – China, the Middle East and parts of France, Germany and Britain.

copper   *tin*

▶ CASTING

Metal items, such as tools and weapons, could be made by casting. The metalworker prepared a stone mould in two parts that fitted together exactly. When joined together and secured with twine, the hollow inside the mould had the shape of the object to be cast. Hot molten metal was poured into the mould through a hole in the top. When the metal had cooled and set, the metalworker took the mould apart to reveal the object. The same mould could be used again and again.

still a problem, however. Metals such as gold and copper were easy to work, but they were soft. They made good adornments, but poor tools. The solution was to combine one metal with another to make an alloy that was hard-wearing. The best alloy discovered in the ancient world was bronze. This was made by mixing copper with a little tin. It was tough, quite easy to work, had a pleasant, golden appearance, and could be sharpened.

Bronze became a popular material for ornamentation, tools and weapons. Sometimes, once a metalworker had smelted some copper and mixed in some tin, he would let the molten metal set into a bar and then hammer it into shape. Liquid metal can also be cast in a mould to produce all sorts of complex shapes. Casting was popular because it was easy to

produce many identical items using the same mould. However, since hammering hardened the metal, this method was still used to make objects like weapons, which had to be very strong.

Metal technology probably began in the Middle East around 3000BC, and spread to other parts of the world during the next 2,000 years. The development of bronzeworking is so important that historians sometimes call this period the Bronze Age. Bronze did not reach all parts of the world. There was no Bronze Age in Australia, South America or many parts of Africa. In such places, although people may have used gold or copper occasionally, they mostly made do with the stone technology they had developed. They had to wait until the coming of iron before they could take full advantage of metals.

▲ THE SPREAD OF COPPER IN EUROPE

In Europe, copper working began in two main areas, Iberia (southern Spain) and the Balkans, where plenty of the metal was available. From these regions, archaeologists have mapped and dated discoveries of bronze objects. This gives a rough idea of how knowledge of the craft spread across the European continent.

Key Dates

- 9000BC Copper used in some parts of Asia for tools and weapons.

- 6000BC Smelting and casting are developed in the Middle East and south-east Europe.

- 4000BC Knowledge of metalworking begins spreading to Europe, Asia and North Africa.

- 3000BC Bronze technology develops in the Middle East.

- 3000–1000BC Better trade routes enable bronzeworking techniques to spread across much of Europe.

- 2000BC Bronzeworking develops in China.

- 2000BC Bronze is used widely in Asia for everyday tools and weapons.

Megaliths

▲ NIGHT SKY
People have always looked to the sky in their religion. Most stone circles and rows of standing stones are arranged to line up with the Sun, Moon or stars.

TOWERING STANDING STONES, massive stone circles, and vast rows of stones are the most awesome of all prehistoric remains. Some of them are so huge that no one knows how Bronze Age people ever managed to build them. Because they are so big, they are known as megaliths, a term that comes from two Greek words meaning huge stones.

Another mystery is exactly what these vast monuments were for. Archaeologists think they may have been used for religious ceremonies. The stones are often lined up with yearly movements of the Sun and stars, so the ceremonies were almost certainly linked to the calendar and the seasons. They may have been fertility ceremonies, relating the crop-growing season to the annual movements of the stars.

There are two famous groups of megaliths in Europe, one on England's Salisbury Plain, the other in Brittany, France. Many of the British monuments are

stone circles, the most famous are at Stonehenge and Avebury. The main monument in Brittany is a series of rows, or alignments, of stones near the village of Carnac. In both cases there are many other prehistoric monuments nearby, such as smaller circles and alignments, earthworks, burial mounds and single standing stones. Together these structures make up

▲ BUILDING STONEHENGE
Stonehenge in Wiltshire, the greatest of all the stone circles, was built with the simplest technology. The builders probably used sleds or rollers to move the stones, each weighing about 40 tons, about 25km/15 miles to the site, before heaving them into place with a combination of ropes and levers.

THE CHANGING MONUMENTS

The megalithic monuments of Europe have stood for thousands of years, but they have not always looked the same. Archaeologists have found many holes in the ground where additional stones and wooden posts once stood, making these sites even more complex than they are today. The monuments were also altered throughout prehistory, with the removal of some stones and the addition of others.

◀ DOLMEN
Groups of stones like this are called dolmens. They started out covered with earth as the chambers of prehistoric burial mounds. When the mound was moved or eroded away, the roof and its supports were left.

▲ CALLANISH STONE CIRCLE
This is quite a small circle of 13 tall, thin stones. It is in the Hebrides off Scotland and is at the focal point of lines of standing stones. The stones, some of which are 4.5m/15ft high, were quarried only a short distance away from the site. Archaeologists have calculated that each of the stones could have been dragged along by about 20 people.

▶ FESTIVAL AT AVEBURY
Another British stone circle, at Avebury in Wiltshire, may been the scene of an annual harvest or farming festival like the one shown here. The form of the ritual is unknown, but there were probably processions, offerings and observations of the stars or Moon.

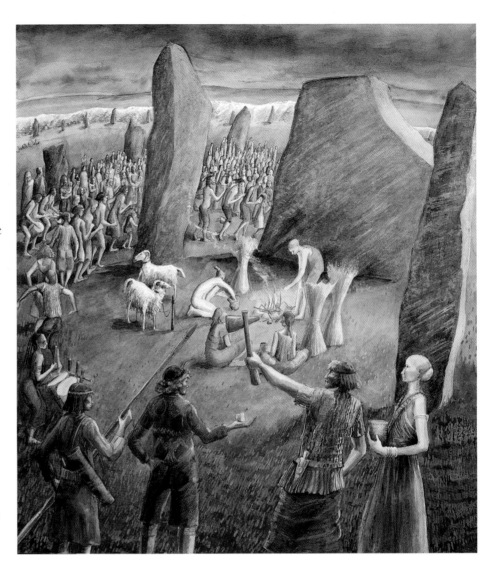

entire regions that would have been known as holy places, landscapes devoted to religion.

The builders of the megalithic monuments had to move and lift huge stones, dig long ditches and pile up enormous mounds of earth. Yet the people of the Bronze Age had no complex machinery, only rollers, levers, ropes and simple hand tools. It must have taken hundreds of people over many years to move the stones. Clearly, a great deal of organization was needed, and probably a ruler with enough power to keep everyone at work on the task. Planning was also important, so that the builders could work out the precise positions for the stones. These vast temples suggest that Bronze Age societies were far more advanced than you would expect, considering the simple tools they had.

◀ MEGALITHIC SITES

Britain, Ireland and northern France are the main areas where megalithic monuments can be found. This probably shows that the people of these three areas were in regular contact, sailing across the English Channel and Irish Sea, when the megaliths were erected. They must have had similar religious beliefs and ceremonies, although we now know very little about these. There were once many more megaliths, but in the 1700s and 1800s farmers cleared away large numbers of these monuments from their fields.

Key Dates

- 4000BC Ditched enclosures common in many parts of Europe.

- 4000BC Long barrows and megalithic tombs become common for high-status burials in Europe.

- 3200BC People in Europe begin to build stone circles.

- 3000BC In Europe, much land is cleared for agriculture.

- 2100BC Stones added to a site originally made up of ditches and earth banks, makes Stonehenge Britain's biggest megalithic site.

- 1500BC The age of stone circles and standing stones comes to an end.

Lake Villages

▲ POTTERY
The lake village people used lots of pottery vessels. Some were narrow-necked, like this jug, which was made for carrying water.

THE SHORES OF ALPINE LAKES in Europe are made up of bogs and marshland. They are difficult to cross and very hard to build on. Yet archaeologists have discovered the remains of several hundred Bronze Age villages in the European Alps. The small settlements with their simple wooden houses were in the middle of swamps by the shores of lakes such as Constance and Neuchâtel, on the borders of modern Switzerland, France and Germany. Why did people put up with damp, boggy conditions?

The lakes themselves were rich in fish, which could be dried or smoked, to preserve them for times when food was less plentiful. Some way beyond the lake shores was grassland, which provided grazing for animals. The foothills of the Alps were thickly forested, offering a good supply of wood for building and fuel. Most important of all, the swampy conditions meant that it very easy to defend the villages against enemies.

Many villages sprang up by the lakes. People cut down trees from the alpine foothills to build their houses. Rooves were thatched with reeds from the lakesides. Each house was raised above the marsh with stout wooden poles rammed deep into the earth. Wood was also used to make pathways across the swamp and to build strong fences around each village. Most villages

TOOLS FOR THE JOB

In prehistoric times, most of the lakeside region of Europe was wooded right down to the lake shores. So, before they could start building homes, the villagers had to clear away some of the trees and prepare logs for building. For this, they needed heavy stone axes with long wooden handles. Once they were settled, they could use lighter metal tools for everyday work in the fields and around the village.

▶ AXE HANDLE
Waterlogged soil near the Swiss lakes has preserved ancient wooden objects, such as this axe handle. This gives us knowledge of craft skills that we lack for most prehistoric peoples.

bronze axehead

bronze sickle

pick

horn toggle

bone amulet

◀ TOOL KIT
After about 2000BC, the alpine lake people started to use bronze to make many of their tools. Axes for chopping and sickles for harvesting were two typical metal items. There were also picks with bone or antler handles.

◀ BONE AND HORN
Many items were made of these materials. Animal horn was a good material to make toggles to fasten coats and tunics. Bone could be carved into all sorts of shapes, including fastenings and pierced objects which may have been sacred charms.

were quite small, with up to 20 houses. Eventually, after 30 or 40 years, the wet ground made the poles supporting the houses rot. Either they were replaced, or the people moved on to another site.

Trapped deep beneath the water, however, an amazing amount of evidence of these villages has been preserved. Archaeologists have brought to the surface some of the timbers from the houses and pathways and bronze implements. In some cases even remains of the people's food and clothing have survived preserved in the cold water.

Some of the settlements had at least one large house. This was probably the home of the village chief. Archaeologists have found decorated bronze weapons and ornaments in these houses, showing that these chiefs were rich and powerful.

▼ ON THE LAKESHORE
This view of a prehistoric lake village shows how close the inhabitants were to the resources they needed to live – reeds and fish in the lake itself, timber from the forests, and fertile fields nearby. For communities like this, easy access to these resources made it worthwhile to build in such a difficult, marshy area.

▲ REEDS
For thatched roofs, by far the best material is reed. It is strong, long-lasting and grows in abundance along the edges of lakes.

▼ LAKESIDE VILLAGE
Sites near lakes have always proved popular in places such as Austria, Switzerland and nearby countries. Places such as Zurich, Neuchâtel, Lausanne and Konstanz are all built by large lakes. Many of these modern towns and cities are built on the sites of prehistoric lake villages. The picture shows a lakeside village in the Austrian Alps. Today, many people like to visit lakeside sites because of the stunning scenery.

Key Dates

- 3000BC Trading villages well established on the shores of the Black Sea; the inhabitants work copper and gold and trade along the local rivers.

- 3000BC People settle along the shores of lakes in Europe's Alpine region.

- 2000BC Substantial wooden villages are built by the settlers in alpine areas. The people purposely select sites that are easy to defend and learn how to fortify their villages with boundary fences.

- 1600BC The heyday of the lake villages comes to an end.

The Iron Age

Bronze was a useful metal, but it was not as hard as stone. Neither was it always easy to find the copper and tin needed to make it. Many people carried on using flint tools and weapons. Then, in around 1300BC, some metalworkers in the Middle East discovered iron.

Iron is a common metal in many parts of the world. It is easy to smelt, providing that the temperature in the furnace is high enough. It can be sharpened easily, and can be strengthened by hammering. When metalworkers first began to smelt iron, they did not realize it was a common material. Because it was new and unusual, it was used for weapons carried by high-ranking men such as chiefs. Soon, however, they saw how common and useful iron was, and began to make iron tools and weapons in large numbers.

Ironworking gradually spread throughout the Middle East and into southern Europe. Iron weapons helped empire-building peoples,

▲ IRON DAGGER
Forged from iron and carried in a bronze sheath, this British dagger probably belonged to an important person such as a chief. It dates from the time when European society was led by warriors.

such as the Hittites of Turkey, to conquer new territory. They helped the Greeks, who were building colonies around the Mediterranean, in much the same way. In India, where the people had found little copper, iron

▼ IRON AGE SETTLEMENT
When the people of Iron Age Europe built a fort, they defended it by building deep ditches. The earth from the ditches was thrown up to make massive banks, giving extra protection. Forts like this covered a huge area, with enough space for people, houses and animals.

REMAINS FROM THE IRON AGE
Many of the most impressive remains from the Iron Age are actually made of bronze. Iron tools and weapons were made in large numbers, but most have rusted away. Bronze objects, on the other hand, are longer lasting, even if buried in the ground. As a result, many bronze items, buried in the graves of high-ranking chieftains, have survived.

◀ ▼ BROOCHES
Iron Age people fastened their clothes with brooches, which were usually made of bronze and could be very ornate. The fibula style had a long pin that worked like a modern safety pin.

fibula brooch

spectacle brooch

▶ LA TÈNE HORN
The curving, swirling lines of the decoration on the end of this horn are typical of the Celtic La Tène style, which developed during the late Iron Age in Europe. It is one of four horns made of bronze found in an Irish lake.

▲ BRONZE SHIELD
A shield, found in Battersea, London, was decorated by hammering the metal to make raised patterns. Bright glass and stones were added.

detail of trumpet end

made metal technology widely available for the very first time.

In Europe, iron transformed people's lives. It enabled the Celtic people, who lived in western Europe, to become warlike and powerful. They built large hill forts, protected by earthworks and fences, and fought off attackers with iron weapons. A whole village could fit into one hill fort, and these forts became bases for warrior chiefs.

The first phase of the European Iron Age is known as the Hallstatt period, after a site in Austria where a number of iron swords were found. Hallstatt chiefs grew rich, both from trading and from forcing people to pay them tribute. Some chiefs even owned goods imported from as far away as Greece and Italy.

After about the 5th century BC, the Celts began to produce metalwork beautifully decorated in a free, swirling style. This style is called La Tène, after the Swiss lakeside site where archaeologists have found many iron and bronze items.

By the time the Romans were building up their empire in Europe, the Celts were powerful enough to fight the Romans' armies and halt them for a while. The Celtic chiefs issued their own coinage, built strong forts and traded with Rome in times of peace. For several centuries, these men of iron were Europe's strongest and most feared leaders.

▲ IRONWORKERS
In order to produce workable iron, the ore (the rock containing the metal) had to be heated to a high temperature. Early ironworkers made kilns of earth to contain the fire so that it could build up enough heat.

▲ IRON AGE SITES
Although Europe has perhaps the most famous of all Iron Age cultures, people in many other parts of the world discovered how to work iron. Eastern Asia and Africa were two areas that had notable Iron Age societies.

Key Dates

- 1300BC Middle Eastern people discover iron and make iron tools and weapons.

- 1000BC Ironworking established in central Europe.

- 800BC Beginning of Hallstatt period.

- 600BC Iron discovered in China; hotter furnaces mean the Chinese can cast iron, something impossible in the west until much later.

- 500BC Ironworking begins in Africa.

- 500BC Ironworking well established in most of Europe.

- 450–100BC Fine metalwork of the La Tène period made in Europe.

The Birth of Civilization

WHILE MANY OF THE EVENTS described so far in this book were happening, another development, more earth-shattering than all the rest, was beginning at different points on the globe. Small towns were growing into cities. Their inhabitants were putting up large temples and palaces, inventing written languages and creating complex societies in which there were many different jobs for people to do. There were farmers, craftworkers, priests, governors and kings. This new city-based way of life is what we now call civilization.

▲ PAINTED POT
Pottery from the Mesopotamian cities is often of a very high quality, thin, well shaped and with elegant decoration.

The place where civilization first began was Mesopotamia, the land between the Tigris and Euphrates rivers in what is now Iraq. This was part of the Fertile Crescent, where farming had started. It was the reliable food supply produced by farming that made the developments that followed possible.

As the farmers became more experienced, they worked out how to irrigate their fields so that they could bring water to the drier areas. This made the food supply more constant. The farmers could also increase

◀ WOMAN AND BABY
This figure of a mother holding a baby is made of clay. It dates from the 'Ubaid period, which lasted from 5500 to 4000BC. At this time, towns were growing into cities, craftworkers were becoming more and more skilled, and local leaders were gaining in power.

the size of their fields by cultivating previously difficult areas.

At the same time, the people of Mesopotamia began to build large, comfortable mud-brick houses. They created beautiful painted pottery, fine clay sculptures, intricate copper implements and elegant adornments with turquoise beads. People from other areas wanted these items, so the Mesopotamians traded with other cultures, carrying their cargo by boat down the rivers and along the Persian Gulf. Gradually, the traders of Mesopotamia became rich and their towns grew into cities. With cities came more power and more complex government. The priests, who were among the most powerful people, built bigger temples, another mark of civilization. Then came writing. At first, this was only a few simple symbols to show who

ARTS OF CIVILIZATION
One of the features of civilization was that society became more complex. In other words, it was divided into more social classes, with more powerful leaders and more difference between rich and poor. The rich people demanded better, more luxurious goods, from pots to ornamentation, and in Mesopotamia this led to the growth of arts and crafts. Pottery, metalworking, building and sculpture are all crafts which developed quickly at this time.

◀ POTTERY FRAGMENTS
Ancient rubbish heaps are treasure troves for archaeologists. Many pieces of broken pottery have been unearthed from the 'Ubaid period, from 5500BC to 4000BC. They often have striking painted decoration.

◀ NECKLACES
Mesopotamian necklaces could have thousands of beads in several separate strings. The large one, found at a farming site called Choga Mami, has around 2,200 beads, crudely shaped from clay.

◀ WRITING
The scribes of Mesopotamia wrote by making marks in clay tablets with a wedge-shaped reed. This writing is called cuneiform, from a Greek word meaning wedge.

▶ HEAD FROM STATUETTE
Terracotta heads like these show the style of sculpture in Mesopotamia, with some features, such as the eyes, enlarged.

owned what. Later people developed more complicated writing systems that people to record stories and religious texts.

The development of writing marks the end of prehistoric society. This happened at different times in different parts of the world. During the lifetimes of some of the prehistoric peoples, civilization was already present in Mesopotamia and other parts of the globe. Civilization came early to the Middle East, Egypt, the Indus Valley in India and parts of China. Elsewhere, in Europe, America and much of Africa, societies based on cities came much later.

In western Europe, for example, it was only with the arrival of the Romans that cities and writing appeared. The Romans took over the area they called Gaul (modern France) in the 1st century BC, some 3,000 years after the first cities were built in Mesopotamia. Today, people in some parts of the world lead successful traditional lifestyles, adapted to their environment just like their prehistoric ancestors. But even they are affected by the decisions of governments and businesses based in the world's cities.

▼ 'UBAID HOUSE
Houses, like this one in modern Iraq, became larger and more complex in the 'Ubaid Period. They were still made of mud-bricks, but had a large central hall, many smaller rooms, a staircase, and drainage into open gullies outside.

Roof of plaster covering rushes on wooden poles

Mud-brick staircase

Main central room

Smoothly plastered floor

Open drain

▲ MARSH ARABS
These Marsh Arabs live in south-eastern Iraq. They herd water buffalo and build houses out of reeds. This traditional lifestyle of the Marsh Arabs existed alongside the growing cities of Mesopotamia.

▼ ZIGGURAT
A Sumerian ziggurat consisted of a stepped platform made of sun-dried mud bricks. Only priests were allowed to climb to the top. An early example of a ziggurat is the White Temple of Uruk, made of white-washed bricks, which dates back to the late 3000s BC.

Key Dates

- 3500BC The first cities are built in Mesopotamia. Among the most important are Uruk and Ur on the banks of the Euphrates River.

- 3200BC Civilization spreads to Egypt.

- 3100BC Writing is developed in and around the city of Uruk; people write on clay tablets.

- 2500BC The first cities are built in the Indus Valley, Pakistan.

- 2300BC Several of the Mesopotamian cities unite as a single kingdom under Sargon of Agade.

- 1800BC Civilization develops separately in northern China.

Glossary

A

alignment Term used to describe objects that are lined up neatly. A stone alignment is a long row of standing stones, often lined up to correspond with the movements of the Sun, Moon or stars.

alloy Material made by mixing two or more metals. The most common alloy in prehistoric times was bronze, made from copper and tin.

archaeologist A person who studies the buildings, tools, pots and other remains of past societies. They dig in the ground looking for objects that provide evidence of how people lived in the past.

archaic Term describing the early stages of development of a species or people. Archaic *Homo sapiens* refers to the remains of our own species that are similar to those of other early hominids.

Australopithecine A hominid of the genus Australopithecus, alive more than a million years ago. They were smaller than later hominids, could stand upright and probably used simple tools.

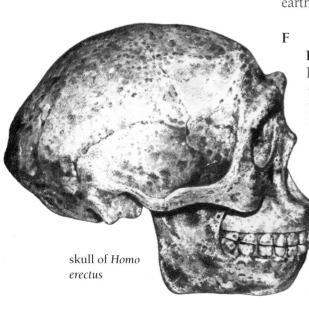

skull of *Homo erectus*

B

Bronze Age Period in which the use of bronze for making tools and weapons became well established (3000–1000BC).

burial mound Artificial earth mound containing human graves.

C

casting Method of making bronze or iron objects by pouring molten metal into a shape, for example an arrowhead.

Celts People who lived in central and western Europe during the Iron Age, just before these areas were occupied by the Romans.

civilization A settled society that has developed writing, organized religion, trade, grand buildings and government.

coiling Technique for making pottery, in which long snake-like coils of clay are wound together and smoothed to make a vessel.

E

earthwork A bank or rampart of earth, often built for protection.

F

Fertile Crescent Area, shaped like a crescent on the map, including modern Israel, Palestine, Syria and parts of Turkey, Iran and Iraq. This was the area in which farming was first established.

fossils Part of an animal or plant that is preserved in stone.

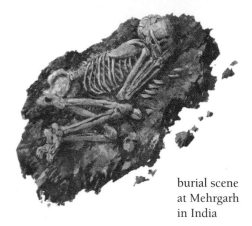

burial scene at Mehrgarh in India

G

genus A group of animals or plants that have characteristics in common. A genus normally has more than one species in it.

glaze Layer of material spread on to a pot before firing to create a hard, waterproof finish.

H

Halstatt Term for the first stage of the Iron Age in Europe, named after an Iron Age site in Austria.

hominid Member of the family Hominidae, which includes humans and australopithecines.

Homo erectus Upright-walking member of the human genus *Homo*, which lived over 500,000 years ago.

Homo habilis Early member of the human genus *Homo*, alive in Africa about 1.7 million years ago.

Homo sapiens The modern human species, which developed around 100,000 years ago, and to which we belong.

hunter-gatherers People who live on meat which they hunt and plants which they gather.

I

Ice Age Period when the temperature was much lower than today, and large parts of the Earth's surface were covered in ice.

Iron Age Period during which iron became the main metal used for tools and weapons, from about 2000BC.

L

La Tène Style of abstract art produced by the Celts, dated around 450–50BC.

land bridge Area of land connecting two landmasses that are now separate.

M

megalith Large stone, standing alone or used as part of a tomb, stone circle or other monument.

Mesolithic The Middle Stone Age. The period during the Stone Age when people improved their hunting techniques and began to make smaller stone tools.

Mesopotamia The fertile area between the Tigris and Euphrates rivers in what is now Iraq, where the earliest civilizations began.

microlith Very small stone cutting blade, often fitted into a wooden handle, typical of the Mesolithic period.

N

Neanderthal Early hominid, shorter and stockier than humans, that lived in Europe and the Middle East and died out around 35,000BC.

gazelle rock art

Neolithic The New Stone Age. The period when people began to farm but were still using stone tools.

O

obsidian Naturally occurring glass-like substance formed in volcanoes. Used in prehistoric times in the same way as flint for making tools.

ore Rock containing deposits of metal.

P

Palaeolithic The Old Stone Age. The period when human life first emerged. This time was typified by a hunter-gatherer way of life and by the use of simple stone tools.

palaeontologist A person who studies fossils.

prehistoric Period before people learnt to write and keep their own historical records. The dates of the prehistoric period vary in different places around the world depending on when people began to develop writing.

pressure flaking The removal of small pieces of stone from the edge of a tool by pushing with a piece of bone or antler. Pressure flaking can produce a finely worked, razor-sharp edge.

woolly rhino

S

scraper Tool used for cleaning animal skins or for carving.

Stone Age Term describing any period when people made their tools and weapons out of stone.

Woman using a scraper to prepare skins for use as clothing and blankets.

Index